Faces from a Good Life

2nd Edition

Faces from a Good Life

A Memoir

Ron Kase

Faces from a Good Life

Copyright © 2022 by Ron Kase

All rights reserved. No part of this publication may be reproduced, distributed, or transmitted in any form without prior permission of the publisher or author, except in the case of brief quotations embodied in critical reviews and certain other uses as permitted by copyright law.

Library of Congress Control Number 202291278

ISBN: 9798839795020

Printed in the United States of America
An Anchor Series 31 Book
Published by Amazon

2nd Edition January 2024

"When people show you who they are, believe them the first time."

Maya Angelou

"The sociology instructor was new. He had come from Boston, He had lived among poets and socialists and Jews and millionaire uplifters at the University Settlement in New York. He led a giggling class through the prisons, the charity bureaus, the employment agencies."

"Main Street" by Sinclair Lewis, published in 1920

Contents

Introduction ix

Chapter 1   Leo McLaughlin, S.J. 1
Chapter 2   The Viking 21
Chapter 3   Why I Love Coffee 31
Chapter 4   The Jewish Atheist Who Enjoys Christmas 43
Chapter 5   Neil O'Connell, OFM 47
Chapter 6   Faces from a Good Life 69
Chapter 7   "The Most Interesting Man in the World" 123
Chapter 8   My Uncle Max 131
Chapter 9   The Irish Connection 143
Chapter 10 Notes of a Frustrated American 161

Books by Ron Kase 189
Author's Page 191

Introduction

Dear Diary, this book is after all, a diary of sorts or a memoir. Its stories are about people whom I knew, and with whom I actually had experiences, and how they have had an effect on my life, in many positive ways. I thank all of them for being who they are and for having a connection with me. I sometimes think I was not worthy of their love, affection, friendship, or even their interest. I have written about people who are not ordinary. Yes, they are smart and talented but, more importantly, they are kind. They are all good listeners who allow others to finish their thoughts without beginning a new comment, proving that they were really listening, and caring about what was just said.

The memoir describes many oddities and obvious emotional conflicts. How does a lifelong Jewish atheist gain the respect and deep friendship, of two Catholic priests, both humanistic and ethical men, who were prominent figures in their respective religious orders? Possibly, because, they clearly understood the complex and terrible issues, both historic and in the present, of their church. I attempt to explain that important part of my life. A lot of the diary is about my family's history, which wasn't my intention in the beginning of the book, but I had fine parents, with little drama, and they loved me, which I wish I had better understood. My grown children, Betsy, Kenneth and Jonathan understand that better than I did.

Kenneth, became ill five years ago, and lost his ability to walk and speak. But speech therapy has helped, and recent surgery has restored his foot to normal, so walking again is a real possibility. I will be grateful always to Natalie, Ken's mother a talented ceramist, who is a phenomenal loving care-giver for our son. Ken, was a well-known jewelry designer and silversmith in Athens, Georgia for twenty-five years until illness settled in his system. Our daughter, Betsy, worked tirelessly when Ken became ill. She arranged for physicians, medical insurance, therapies, medications, and home care for him. She also led the funding of an endowed scholarship in Kenneth's name, in the art school of the University of Georgia where Kenneth, had earned an MFA degree. Betsy published a book titled "Porch Arrangements" that contains photographs of her brother's creations taken over the years he lived in Athens, Georgia.

Betsy is an entrepreneur who opened a yoga center over twenty-one years ago and created Westchester County's two best rated yoga places that were called *Yoga Haven*. She had the constant support of husband David, an exceptionally competent financial advisor, and my favorite son-in-law. David lost his mother earlier this year. Helaine Rossett was a delightful person, and always fun to be with.

Along with offering yoga classes for everyone, Betsy certified new yoga instructors after a yearlong course and found programs, and distributed products leading to better health, which she offered to her loyal clients. After the frustration of Covid's disastrous effect on her business, Betsy is planning a new enterprise, in partnership with a former student who became a good friend. They are developing a new modern Yoga space in a former industrial building in Tuckahoe, NY.

Kathleen, my wife of thirty-two years is almost twenty years younger than I am, which means we won't grow old together, but our time together has been wonderful in many ways. She is so smart and so good to everyone. Kathleen's love of travel, which I have embraced, has inspired her to create a successful company called *BestKase Travel LLC* that had grown significantly prior to Covid. The greatest gift of our relationship is our son Jonathan's presence in our lives, which is immeasurable, in the joy he has produced for us. Jonathan, graduated with honors from the University of Tampa, one of the most competent universities that I have ever gotten to know. Upon graduation he promptly decided to enter graduate studies, and was accepted to the full time Public Administration program of the City University of New York at Baruch College. Jonathan excelled in the 45 credit Master's program, and just prior to his graduation was employed by the Cardozo School of Law as a development officer, and advanced to Assistant Director of Development. After a successful three and a half years at Cardozo, Jonathan was recruited by Cambridge America. He now represents, England's Cambridge University through out the United States meeting regularly with the university's impressive alumni.

I also have a wonderful grandson Jonah, Betsy and David's son. He's a sophomore at Drexel University and a design major. He's extremely talented and creative following his mom and Uncle Kenneth. I must admit, that I didn't spend as much time with Jonah when he was younger because our Jonathan is just seven years older than Jonah, and we spent almost every weekend, for many years at Jonathan's baseball, soccer, basketball games, and tournaments. We loved doing that but, I lost good times with my grandson, which I hope we are making up for now to some degree. During Covid's worst time Jonah took a leave from Drexel, and joined an organized group of college students, all from the Northeast. They traveled safely to the Southwestern section of the United States, and spent time on Native American Reservations learning about the problems faced by native people.

The group also travelled to the southern border, a hot bed of political issues and human misery, made even more terrible by the Trump administration. Jonah's travel group saw towns in desert country that had only one small place to buy food. They learned about the great water supply issue, and the fragile family farms trying to hold on in the age of agribusiness. The academic part of the tour required written work analyzing each experience that earned college credit from Portland State University. The group made most of their meals, cooking and serving, and eating communally, and Jonah became a competent chef. For the second part of that year, Jonah went to Israel with another group of college students, and travelled all over seeing the good and the not so good of the Jewish nation. He was there during the series of missile strikes by Hamas on Israel. Of course, Jonah or anyone else could not have anticipated the terrible attack on innocents by Hamas in October of this year, and the subsequent war between Israel and Humas that produces more innocent victims daily. His experiences in Israel were definitive and maturing. Central to his development, as a competent and caring adult is Ava, his lovely girlfriend from their earliest days at college. Ava is a dance therapy major at Drexel, and together they make a delightful, well intentioned, healthy life style couple. Jonah, has returned to Drexel to complete his degree where he has attained a place on the Dean's List for his outstanding interior design work. He has also become expert in the fabrication of architectural metal structures used in residential and commercial spaces.

 Last December I had surgery to correct a kidney and bladder issue that suddenly appeared, and was discovered by my good friend and physician Dr. Richard Lucanie. The surgery that some in the medical field believed would not be successful was performed robotically over seven hours by Dr. Gregory Joice, and Dr. Preston Kerr, at Columbia University Medical Center in New York City. The procedure was totally successful thanks to the skill and determination of the surgeons. My gratitude to them is boundless, and their attention to me over the six days at Columbia was inspiring and healing due to the kindness of the entire team including the outstanding, talented and humanistic surgical residents. Recently I met up with Dr. Joice and Dr. Kerr, for my last post-surgery appointment. I hugged both of them, and told them how much their agreeing to perform the surgery has meant to me. I had sent thank you letters to them previously, which they shared with the resident doctors, whom had taken such good care of me, for the time I was hospitalized. Dr. Joice, said that his mentor at Harvard told him, "We're not in this for the money, but some gratitude is nice." We thanked each other, and I left feeling as though it was one of the best days of my life.

    I wrote this book as a review of my life, which all in all has been good hence the title, "Faces from a Good Life," which is kind of a diary that I have wanted to write for a long time. Some of the people with whom I have been closest, and have loved their friendships have passed away, and this is the way I have memorialized them. The last section, "Notes of a Frustrated American" is my way of dealing with the, Republican's Taliban, attack on our nation, as they follow happily and blindly, the insurrectionist traitor, the degenerate, criminal, moron, Donald J. Trump. Every day since he was somehow elected in 2016, I wake up hoping that the news was reporting his death. I'm not being harsh or hateful, but patriotic. I am literally worried about our country's survival, as we may not continue as a democracy, where election results were always valid, which used to be important to everyone. America's, white evangelicals are determined to establish a single party system in the United States similar to the dictatorships in Russia and Hungary. In fact the American Conservative Political Action Conference, which is dominated by evangelicals was held in Dallas recently with Hungary's dictator Victor Orban, as the keynote speaker. And, they are not embarrassed by inviting, and featuring a fascist, to an American political organization's annual event. As Benjamin Franklin said, "It's a republic, if we can keep it."

Revised January 2024

CHAPTER 1

Leo McLaughlin, S.J.

THE *NEW YORK Times* of Saturday December 14, 1968 reported on its front page that FATHER LEO MCLAUGHLIN had resigned as the president of Fordham University. McLaughlin was the most recognizable and charismatic of all of the city's university presidents. The accompanying photo showed the handsome, square jawed, McLaughlin wearing the traditional black suit and white collar of a Roman Catholic priest. In fact, Leo McLaughlin, was a member of the Jesuit order, the church's intellectual and usually politically liberal, society of priests. The Jesuit magazine *America* is known as a journal of thoughtful commentary focused on social justice.

The *Times* article didn't give a reason for Father McLaughlin's resignation from Fordham. After all he was responsible for building the university's Lincoln Center campus, after raising millions of dollars for the project. What it did say was that McLaughlin would act as the university's Chancellor for a while, before taking up residence, as a Visiting Scholar at Johnson C. Smith College in North Carolina, a historically black institution, now a university, founded under the auspices of the Presbyterian Church, in Charlotte in 1867 as a "Freeman's school." Another *Times* article on May 28, 1970, written by Andrew H. Malcolm, had as its headline, "Fordham Chancellor takes Post at Negro College."

Leo Plowden McLaughlin was born in to a prominent family in New York City in 1912. His father was an attorney. His mother managed the family's four-story Brownstone house in Manhattan, directing a cook and two serving girls from Ireland. Leo attended Loyola Prep in Manhattan run by the Jesuits, and then Georgetown University, and for his junior year, the Sorbonne in Paris. Leo's family spent summers in France, and he returned to Paris after graduation from Georgetown, and his joining the Society of Jesus, known as the Jesuit order, to study at the University of Paris for a doctorate in the Humanities.

Leo moved quickly within the Jesuit order, teaching and occupying various staff positions at Fordham University, and after nine years was appointed president of St. Peter's University in Jersey City, another Jesuit college. McLaughlin spent only a year at St. Peters before he was appointed President of Fordham. Possibly the most significant event of his year in New Jersey, at St. Peter's was attending a formal dinner party at the Upper Montclair estate of the Gombos family, in support of St. Peter's University. He returned several times as a dinner guest becoming a friend of the family, which included two elementary school children, both girls. Twenty years later, Sari Gombos, age 26 would marry Leo McLaughlin.

Leaving Fordham, McLaughlin left behind a life to which he had been committed since high school. Was it a mid-life crisis, a crisis of faith, boredom, loneliness, or a need to be responsible only to one's self? McLaughlin wasn't sure. He didn't regret his decision, but didn't know what he wanted to do with his life. Leo was highly intellectual, disarmingly charming, and brilliant in every area of the Humanities and the Social Sciences, but he became lost and lonesome while living in North Carolina. He resided on the Johnson C. Smith University campus, in an apartment carved out of a stately old house. Leo, had never prepared a meal or dealt with mundane activities such as doing his laundry, or shopping for groceries. He quickly learned what he needed to do, and developed a routine, but soon he became bored with the slower life in Charlotte. Leo had met and known New York City's leading members of the intellectual and business worlds, and the arts and politics. He regularly dined at expensive charitable events, private dinners held at the city's most fashionable addresses, or meals at Cipriani with his close friend Leon Lowenstein. Now he usually dined alone, either in the student cafeteria or a make shift meal of his own creation. On weekends McLaughlin often was invited to the homes of faculty members or the university's president the friend who took him in when Leo left New York. He appreciated the kindness of the faculty members and their families, and enjoyed his interactions with the students. They all tried to make him feel welcome, but Leo, confused and unhappy realizing that his time at Johnson C. Smith, now almost two years, was coming to an end.

While at Johnson C. Smith, Leo had occasional contact with some former Catholic priests he had known in New York. Oddly, several were members of the faculty of a new state college in northern New Jersey that was struggling to emulate the academic structure of England's Oxford University. The college's founding president, an Englishman, had been a minor administrator at Oxford. He knew absolutely nothing about creating an American public college, especially the political machinations of state finance, but was hired anyway by an inexperienced and naïve board of trustees. The new president insisted the center of the academic program was to be the Oxford like Tutorial Program, in which students were assigned reading in the humanities and the social sciences using The Great Books. Students would meet individually with faculty members for discussions and analysis. Unfortunately, the college's students were more traditional, and expected classes and courses found in the other colleges in the region. Only the physical and biological sciences were presented in the usual college level manner. The college's administrators tried to emulate Oberlin, Swarthmore, or Reed academically, but were unsuccessful, and the new institution was floundering. Some of the former Catholic priests, now faculty members, insisted on contacting, Leo McLaughlin, to offer him the position of savior and Director of the Tutorial Program.

The offer from New Jersey came at the perfect time for McLaughlin. While he appreciated the safe haven Johnson C. Smith University had provided him for the last two years, he wanted to return to the New York area. He was intrigued by the campus to which he was headed as it was the place where Daniel and Philip Berrigan had hidden out while the FBI was searching for them. Daniel Berrigan, a Jesuit priest, and Philip Berrigan, a Josephite priest were anti-Viet Nam War activists who burned draft board files, and led other acts of civil disobedience against the unpopular war in Asia. Along with the brothers hiding in an empty dorm section was Elizabeth McAlister, a Catholic nun, and member of the faculty of Marymount College in Tarrytown, NY. She was also on the FBI's most wanted list for burning draft records in Catonville, Maryland. Eventually Elizabeth and Philip Berrigan married, had three children, and spent a third of their married years in court or in jail.

McLaughlin, arrived in New Jersey in 1973, and was welcomed by the cadre of expriests and liberal faculty members, who treated him like a celebrity. Like every challenge he ever undertook in his life, McLaughlin committed himself completely to the program he was hired to create. He resumed some of the friendships he had made while Fordham's president, but not all of the people in his past were happy to hear from him. Some conservative Catholics at Fordham and among its alumni, would not forgive Leo for taking down the crucifixes in every Fordham University classroom.(1)

The state college's campus was a lively place. Another well-known Catholic priest Father Harry Browne was also part of the informal faculty life of the college. Fr. Browne was pastor of St. Gregory's RC Church on Manhattan's West side. In fact, Daniel Berrigan was arrested at the church after being hidden there. Harry Browne was a fiery advocate of affordable housing, who was frequently on television news programs castigating New York's Governor Nelson Rockefeller and Mayor John Lindsey. However, Fr. Browne, was often seen on campus attending faculty events due to his unapproved and unimaginable marriage to Dr. Flavia Alaya a humanities professor, and a member of the college's founding faculty. The couple had three children. Describing the funeral mass at St. Gregory's Church for Harry Browne in 1980, Flavia Alaya wrote, "The mass was celebrated by the Bishop of New York, twenty priests, his three children and his concubine." (*Under the Rose,* Flavia Alaya. The Feminist Press)

Certainly, the most important person with whom Leo McLaughlin, reunited with was Sari Gombos who had been a child the last time they were together. McLaughlin's former secretary at Fordham had contacted him to say that Sari had asked her where Leo was, and if she could speak with him. He readily agreed, and they began to talk on the phone almost daily until they planned to meet in Manhattan for dinner. Sari Gombos was an intelligent, attractive woman, a graduate of Trinity College in Washington, DC, and a devoted Roman Catholic. She had grown up in a wealthy family and had a polished, but approachable manner, and worked as a freelance writer contributing to several monthly magazines on a regular basis. Leo felt an intense emotional attraction to Sari, and for the first time in his life, knew he was in love. Sari admitted that she felt the same way about Leo, and after a year of seeing each other they married in a quiet ceremony in Elkton, Maryland in June of 1975. Technically McLaughlin was still a Jesuit priest. He had resigned from Fordham, not from the order. Leo, had not been laicized the process whereby a Catholic priest was returned to layman status. Leo decided not to undergo the process, and was in his mind a married priest, but in actuality had been excommunicated. In September, Leo and Sari announced their marriage setting off news headlines in certain media outlets.

Leo & Me

How did I an Associate Professor of undergraduate Human Services, in a CUNY college, develop an almost father/son relationship with Leo McLaughlin a giant of intellectualism with great accomplishments, and recognized by almost everyone connected to higher education in the Northeast? I'm going to tell you. In 1966, I was the Associate Director of the anti-poverty program in lower Westchester County. I had earned a Master's degree in Educational Sociology at NYU. Something in the Sunday *New York Time,* advertisement called me to apply for a position as Community Program developer at New York City College of Technology in Brooklyn the former New York City Community College that had become a four-year college, and boasted an enrollment of 18,000 students. I applied, and was accepted for the position and was appointed an Assistant Professor. After two years I was appointed Chairman of a new department called Human Services. We offered degrees in social welfare work, and elementary teacher education, and a two-year degree in early childhood for pre-school staff.

At the time, the federal government funded urban students studying for degrees in the human services. I put together an excellent faculty in each area, and we developed the curriculum for the disciplines. The faculty was young, bright, and ambitious, and the students, mostly woman, were older, smarter, and tougher, so we had to be very good teachers to stay ahead of them. I was tenured in three years, and promoted, and told that without a doctorate, I would not go any further in the CUNY system.

Actually the CUNY pay scale was terrible, but I went back to NYU, and asked my former faculty advisor, DR. FRED REDEFER, to accept me into the doctoral program in Educational Sociology. He did, even after my poor showing on the math section of the GRE. However, at the end of the academic year Dr. Redefer the only sociologist at the time looking at the long-term effects of rapid population growth on higher education, retired. I was left at the mercy of a new department chairman who clearly believed I didn't belong there because I was a part-time student with a full-time position. Nevertheless, I accumulated credits for three years avoiding my advisor as much as I could, and teaching a full program while chairing the department at CUNY.

One day while at lunch, at Manhattanville College in Purchase, NY my friend DR. ELIZABETH MCCORMACK the college's president listened patiently as I complained about my lack of progress toward the doctorate at NYU. Elizabeth McCormack had been a Catholic nun, a Madame of the Sacred Heart, a French order, with a mission some said for wealthy Catholic girls. The Kennedy sisters were Manhattanville graduates. Elizabeth was a highly respected educator and leader. She had recently resigned from her order, and changed the structure of Manhattanville College from a Catholic college for girls from prominent Catholic families to a private co-ed college for anyone meeting the admission requirements. Therefore Elizabeth was someone to listen to, and that day I certainly did. She asked if I knew of a new experimental program, based at Antioch College in Yellow Springs, Ohio. I did not. Elizabeth, said she had been approached to become involved in the experimental Ph.D. program at Antioch called the, Union Graduate School, sponsored by the University Without Walls program, but had declined due her own uncertain situation at Manhattanville College. It was the first program of its kind, and it was an attempt to discover whether or not the advanced academic degree may be earned through a different kind of preparation. Elizabeth, made a phone call on my behalf, and a few days later I received, in the mail, an extensive application to the new doctoral program. About one year later Elizabeth McCormack left Manhattanville College, and became the advisor for philanthropy to the Rockefeller family. She married Jerry Aron an accountant who was divorced and Jewish. Sometime later Elizabeth, agreed to be the external reader on my committee, and when I visited her at 30 Rockefeller Center the walls of the corridors leading to her office were covered with original paintings by Matisse, Renoir, Monet and Degas.

I completed the application, and wrote a long biographical essay, and collected four strong recommendations from Dr. Elizabeth McCormack, Dr. Fred Redefer, who had retired from NYU, Dr. Leon Goldstein the dean of my college, and someone else whose name I have forgotten. I was accepted along with fifteen other applicants, and invited to a two-week long colloquium in Yellow Springs, Ohio, in June on the campus of Antioch College. The college was founded in 1850 by America's leading liberal educator Horace Mann who remained at the college as president, for the rest of his life. Horace Mann is the father of America's system of public education. He believed, which at the time was a radical idea, in education for everyone, including Black people, Native Americans and women.

There was something almost magical about the Antioch campus, in those days. It was a highly selective Liberal Arts college concentrating on social justice, where the concept of co-op education was born. We stayed in Birch Hall, a cubist style structure designed by the famed international architect Eero Saarinen in 1948. Orientation was conducted by Samuel Baskin a psychologist and educational reformer from NYU. He made the point that while we were guests of Antioch College, and paid tuition to Antioch, our program was independent and sponsored by almost twenty colleges and universities in the University Without Walls (UWW) program. That was just as well as Antioch College began to unravel in the following years, and had closed, and then reopened several times, a sad ending for one of America's most unique colleges.(2)

Faculty members arrived two days later. I was shocked when Margaret Mead America's most important cultural anthropologist spoke to our small group for an entire day with never a moment that wasn't fascinating. Following Margaret Mead, during the next week were Goodwin Watson the noted psychologist and humanist from Columbia University, Roy Fairfield of Harvard, the eminent Maine historian, the poet Elizabeth Sewell, of Fordham University, Robert Hutchins from the University of Chicago, and Leo McLaughlin. There were others I'm certain, but once I met Leo, I didn't care who else was there. Each of the faculty members had pledged to act as doctoral advisor for one or two students, and Leo said, I was the only student he would accept from the group.

Over the next four years I saw Leo two or three times a month. We had agreed that my thesis topic would be a review of the literature concerning the utopian communities in America in the 19th century. Leo and I discussed the topic endlessly, and I researched and read everything I could find about the communities that promised a new kind of life a, "Heaven on Earth" for its members. Mainly I used the facilities of the

Gould Library at the University Heights campus of NYU. As an alum, I had free access to the material. I researched and wrote papers, which became chapters on the Transcendentalists of Brook Farm, the Jewish Am Olam, New Harmony, the Oneida Community, Amana Colonies, Oberlin Colony and the oldest community, really an off-shoot religion the Shakers. Leo urged me to take a graduate class in the subject, but after a thorough search of colleges in the area, I was unable to find a suitable course. So Leo, suggested I develop a course on utopian communities myself, and offer it through my department at CUNY. I did, and taught a section every semester until I left the college to become an administrator at Fairleigh Dickinson University in New Jersey.

The Union Graduate School doctoral candidates met two or three times a year, in a colloquium to share research and progress and problems. We presented our work to a usually highly critical audience. The most memorable meeting as far as I was concerned was held at, Echard College in St. Petersburgh, Florida, led by Dr. Goodwin Watson, of Columbia University. Dr. Watson's message to us was, "Never be ordinary."

Leo had the use of an office at The College Board the non-profit college association that owns the SAT examinations. Ironically the Board at that time was located on 9th Avenue at 60th Street, directly across from Fordham University's Lincoln Center campus that Leo had conceived, developed, and built. Frustrated with the administration at the state college, he had left the position believing something else would open up for him. I would meet him in Manhattan with my written work, a journal of my academic activities, and other events, and we would discuss my research and plans for the future. Leo was an exacting critic of written material, and I did not get used to his rapid scanning of my work, his comments written in red, and his semi approval statement, "Well, your writing is getting better." It actually was getting better, and I became known as a good writer, through which I have had a fine career, thanks to Leo's persistence. One day in the tiny office Leo seemed perturbed when I arrived. He explained that he was writing an article about the theory of the universe as put forth by the ancient Greek philosopher Democritus, and was searching the original Greek in order to be certain his understanding was completely accurate. That was Leo. Besides Greek he knew Latin, of course, also Hebrew, French, Spanish and Italian.

My thesis was accepted, and a final meeting of my committee was scheduled, and held at NYU. It wasn't a defense, but a discussion of philosophy and ideas. Attending was Leo, Elizebeth McCormack, two NYU professors, one a sociologist, the other a social psychologist, and a fellow doctoral candidate.

Leo and Sari purchased a small Cape Cod style home, on Radcliff Street in Wyckoff, New Jersey. They each had an office, Sari's upstairs and Leo's on the first floor. They had a busy social life with Sari attempting, and succeeding to create a salon in their small living room. I was at their home regularly now that I had finished my degree work. Leo introduced me to the Italian aperitif Campari, which is distilled rhubarb and herbs. The drink is dark red and bitter, but over ice with a lemon wedge is delicious. It's the only liquor I enjoy. Leo enjoyed all wines, and imbibed every day with dinner. However, each year for the entire month of January, Leo would not have a single drink containing alcohol, in order to prove to himself that he was not an alcoholic. Sari, however didn't observe the January period of prohibition.

Interesting people showed up at the McLaughlin home, usually on the weekends. Frequent visitors were, Howard Radest and his wife Rita. Radest, was the executive director of the, American Ethical Union, the parent organization of the Ethical Culture humanist movement. Bob Cassidy philosophy professor and former seminarian, always interesting and entertaining, was there. Elizabeth McCormack, and Jerry Aron, who were recently married would enjoy the good food and conversation along with writers from Sari's career in New York's magazine world, and Pat Sexton, the NYU sociologist, with her husband Brenden of the UAW, and editor Barbara Epstein were some of the luminaries who made their way to Wyckoff. The modest Cape Cod at times seemed to be transformed into a fashionable assemblage of intellectualism with the lights low and candles illuminating just enough of the guest's faces. Discussions were brilliant or silly, free and contrived, and always respectful. One evening Leo opened a bottle of brandy from the time of Napoleon. It had been a gift to him while president of Fordham. I don't remember the brandy's taste or bouquet, but everyone agreed it was a great occasion. I believe that providing the perfect place, for his good friends, was the best time of Leo's life.

Leo decided he would write about his observations and impressions of various parts of the society and our culture. However, there wasn't a market for his work. I had published his article "Aging" in my first book *The Human Services,* but his material kept getting rejected. He had happily given up the full-time position at the state college because he was bored and believed that he could collect Social Security. Sari, had an inheritance from her parents, but some of that was used to buy their home along with a loan from Leo's sister in California. Leo confided to me that he had less than seven years of employment outside of the Jesuit order. At the time, Catholic orders of priests, brothers and nuns didn't pay into the Social Security system, which left countless retired clergy penniless, and dependent on their families to support them.

I decided to call Father Tim Healy the president of Georgetown the Jesuit's most prestigious university. Healy had been Vice Chancellor of CUNY prior to being appointed to the presidency of Georgetown, and was Executive Vice President, during Leo's presidency of Fordham. I had met him once through a faculty colleague, but knew he would not remember me. At the time, I was the assistant provost of the Fairleigh Dickinson University campus that sprawled between Teaneck and Hackensack in New Jersey. I called Georgetown, and left word that I was a friend of Leo McLaughlin, and had to speak with Father Healy. Leo had always spoken with affection and respect for Tim Healy so I believed my calling him for help was the correct thing to do. About two hours later a worried sounding Tim Healy returned my call himself, and asked what was wrong? I assured him that Leo was well, but in need of money, since he didn't have the requisite forty quarters of paid full-time work that is required to collect Social Security payments. Father Healy listened to my explanation, and without any hesitation said, "All right, Georgetown will pay into Leo's account in the system, as if he had been on staff here. The Jesuits owe him that much. I will take care of everything and will inform Leo. Thank you for calling me."(3)

At age seventy-nine, while vacationing with Sari in the Canary Islands Leo suffered a stroke. Returning home was a nightmare, an ambulance transported him to the old Kessler Rehabilitation Institute in West Orange, NJ. Sari called me as soon as she was home and got herself together. I immediately drove to Kessler and sat with Leo for several hours. He was unable to speak clearly and his right side was mostly affected. He stayed at Kessler for several weeks, and I visited many times always trying to be cheerful. When I left him, I'd sit in my car and cry. It hurt as much as if it were my own dear father, sick and helpless. Leo struggled at home, for more than two years, while Sari grew distant and resentful. Except for preparing meals, Sari was away from the house or in her upstairs office.

I had married again, and we lived in Ramsey, NJ a town adjacent to

Wyckoff. Sari would sometimes call in the evening, and we'd talk for an hour or more. But, then the calls came later and it was obvious she had been drinking. During my visits to their house Sari would talk to me out of Leo's hearing of her regrets, fears and depression. One day the phone in my office rang, and it was my wife Kathleen. She said a police officer from Wyckoff had called our home and needed to speak to me. I called the phone number he had left, and was connected to a police sergeant. He explained that my name and number in Ramsey, in the McLaughlins' phone book, were the closest to Wyckoff and asked if I would please come to the McLaughlin home as soon as possible.

I left my office at the local college, and raced to Radcliff Street believing that Leo had died. However, upon entering the house, there was Leo sitting on the blue couch in the living room. We embraced, and I looked questionably at the two police officers standing nearby. One went to find the sergeant I had spoken to on the phone. I still didn't understand the situation. The sergeant asked if I knew Mrs. McLaughlin. I answered, "Of course I know her. Where is she?" He gestured for me to follow him upstairs. In Sari's office a white sheet covered a shape on the floor. It was Sari and she was dead.

Leo stayed at the Christian Health Center that night. The Center is a well-regarded residential facility for persons with physical and mental health issues. I promised to see him in the morning, and later that day a doctor from the Center called asking me to meet with him at 9 am the next day. I did, and explained who Leo was and what had happened to him. Four days later, Kathleen and I picked up Leo to go to the funeral home for Sari's wake arranged by a priest of their church, St. Elizabeth's in Wyckoff. Bob Cassidy had called all of Leo's friends, and many were there. I had called Bob the day Sari died, and he asked if it was self-inflicted. I said I didn't know, and to this day I still don't know if Sari facing great challenges mixed pills and alcohol as an answer to her problems. It was rumored that Sari's sister would show up, but she didn't appear.

Suddenly all attention in the funeral home was centered on the ten black suited Jesuits, who had arrived from Fordham University to honor Leo. I had just finished an unhappy conversation with Leo's niece, his sister's daughter, her husband, and their twenty-year-old daughter. They had come from California. Leo's sister had passed away a few years prior. They wanted to know, if Leo was incompetent, who would control his assets. I assured them I didn't know, but as far as I knew Leo had few, if any assets. Bob Cassidy interrupted us saying, "I have an idea, come with me and back up what I say." We approached the priest who was the rector of the Jesuit community at Fordham. He was friendly, and Bob asked me to talk about Leo since he had left Fordham almost twenty years earlier. Before I could finish, the rector said, "We will take him. He can live in Murray-Weigel, our residence for the fathers, who need to be in a medical setting." Bob asked about financial arrangements, and was told, there would not be any. "Leo McLaughlin will be back with the Jesuits." We thanked the rector and Bob said, "you tell the family. I can't abide them. I'll tell Leo."

I found Leo's family in another room, and explained the generous offer from the Jesuit rector. Their reaction was not unexpected. His niece said, "No, they will take the house and car, and their joint bank account, and I don't know what else." I assured the California relatives that the Jesuits didn't want anything that belonged to Leo, not even his Social Security. They calmed down and agreed that Leo could return to Fordham, if they could put his house up for sale before they left to go home to California. I urged them to talk with an attorney and a realtor, and reminded them I had to make sure that Leo's possessions were saved, and I would bring them to Fordham. They calmed down and said they would give my name and phone number to the realtor. After Sari's funeral I collected Leo's personal possessions, clothing, many photos, and small pieces of furniture, his bed spread, pillows, and wall hangings to decorate his room. Several of Leo's friends helped bring everything to the Bronx campus.

Two months after Leo entered Murray-Weigel, I received a call from a real estate broker in Wyckoff who said that the family had hired a company to clean out the house, in order to get it ready for sale. If I wanted to save anything belonging to Leo or Sari, I had to get there right then. Once again I raced to Radcliff Street, and stopped the tossing out of Leo's life. I told the crew to remove only furniture and carpet, drapery and the kitchen items. I began to look through Leo's papers, books and memorabilia. It was impossible to read everything so I loaded the boxes into my SUV for later scrutiny. I found Leo's diplomas, degrees, the silver chalice, the paten, silver cruets and ciborium, all required for the Catholic mass, dozens of fine art books, hundreds of photos, and his Fordham Club beer stein with Father Leo on the rim. Also found was a book of impressionist paintings signed by every member of the St. Peter's University faculty, given to Leo when he left there. I will return the book to St. Peters one day. I didn't take anything that had belonged to Sari. All these years later I still have Leo's possessions in our attic, carefully packed up except for his Fordham Club stein, which is on my dresser so I can see it every day and think about Leo. He passed away in August 1996 at age 84.

In March 2022, Fordham University appointed, Dr. Tania Tetlow, as its president, the first non-Jesuit and a woman. Leo McLaughlin would have applauded.

My Favorite Leo McLaughlin Stories

One day at lunch with Leo in Manhattan, he enjoyed the hamburgers served at O'Neal's Balloon, a restaurant across from Lincoln Center, he looked wistfully across to the eight-acre Fordham University campus at Lincoln Center. He said, "See that long building across campus from the law school?" Well, that's the Leon Lowenstein Center, the main academic building, and the largest structure ever built by Fordham." Our lunches were served, interrupting Leo's story. Later he continued, "Leon Lowenstein was my closest friend, when I was president. We had dinner together three or four times a week. His wife was ill and bed ridden so he welcomed having a dinner companion. He liked Cipriani so we went there a lot. Leon was the owner of the largest textile company in the country making bed sheets and towels, drapery, table covers, and other cloth products."

Leo hesitated, had a sip of his draft beer, and continued, "One morning Leon called my office and said to me, Leo there's a war on. It was June 1967, and Israel had been attacked by Egypt, Syria, and Jordon. Leon asked for a contribution from the Jesuits to aid Israel in its war effort. I had a check for $10,000 prepared, and delivered by messenger to Leon's office before noon that day." Leo smiled before continuing the story. "A few weeks later, Leon Lowenstein made the largest ever contribution to Fordham."

The State of New York, feeling generous in 1966, made three grants to institutions of higher education, in New York City. The grants were the first of their kind, for a one-year residency by a noted scholar. The grant to CUNY brought historian Arthur Schlesinger, Jr. to New York, where he remained until retiring. The grant to NYU brought the Irish diplomat and gadfly Conner Cruise O'Brien, to the Washington Square campus, and the grant to Fordham attracted Marshall McLuhan, Canadian philosopher and media theorist, whose theme "The medium is the message," was popular among anti-print intellectuals, college students, and television personalities. Leo McLaughlin had personally contacted McLuhan, and closed the deal with the elusive Canadian. Leo hoped McLuhan's presence would shake up some of the staid and satisfied Fordham professors, however, a phone call from Louis J. Lefkowitz, Attorney General of New York, threatened his plan. "Leo, Louie Lefkowitz here. New York law says you can't have the money for McLuhan. Fordham is a Jesuit controlled university. Your board has all priests on it. I'm sorry."

Leo was shocked, "Louie, McLuhan is on his way here from Toronto. I have a suite reserved for him at the mid-town Sheraton, and Louie you're an alumnus of Fordham." The next day, Leo began to expand Fordham's board of trustees. He eased off more than half of the board's Jesuit members, and replaced them with influential people who were not necessarily Catholics. He had the crucifixes removed from every classroom wall, and he opened up the curriculum, in order to encourage experimentation, and Leo paid McLuhan with contributed funds, for his year as a scholar in residence at Fordham University. (4)

(1) The *Fordham University Alumni Newsletter* printed this tribute to Leo McLaughlin. "Some maintain that Leo McLaughlin was the Jesuit's answer to a time of intellectual and social ferment. Others insist that he was merely his own man. While he shocked certain Jesuits, students, and alumni with frequency, the Jesuits at Fordham and the entire Fordham community loved Leo and he loved them. After service as one of the most caring faculty members and as one of the most successful deans in the history of Fordham College, the University appointed Fr. McLaughlin president in 1965. As remembered by *The New York Times,* he was "a transforming president....he opened up the curriculum beyond the traditional theological courses, encouraged academic experimentation, fought for higher faculty salaries....turned the established Jesuit faculty inside out....and even wrested the University from Jesuit control." In 1969, so that

Fordham would qualify for state aid, Leo restructured the board of trustees so that it no longer consisted mostly of Jesuits, for the first time a majority of the trustees were members of the laity (and some were not even Catholic). Leo recomposed religious studies as an academic pursuit rather than a method of doctrinarian and ordered icons removed from prominent areas on campus. For the first time in the history of the University, Leo applied the same criteria for tenure and promotion to both Jesuits and lay faculty, and he began to establish academic chairs for the faculty. Still later in 1969, after one of the most dynamic tenures of any president of an American university, Leo left the presidency of the University and assumed the role of chancellor, a fund-raising position. Later, he left Fordham to resume his academic career at Johnson C. Smith University. During the 1970's, Leo applied for and received a release from his vows. In 1975, at the age of 61, Leo announced that he had married Sari Gombos, a writer he had met several years earlier. After the death of his wife in 1994, Leo needed full-time medical care. Aware of Leo's need, in an act of love, the very Jesuits, whom he had challenged on so many occasions, insisted that he be admitted to the Jesuit infirmary at Fordham, where he spent his last months surrounded by friends, contemporaries and classmates. Rev. Joseph A. O'Hare, S.J., the University president, and Rev. Joseph A. Novak, S.J., the rector of the Jesuit community, celebrated Leo's funeral mass in the University Church with a large number of Jesuit brothers."

(2) The Union Graduate School lasted only sixteen years. The doctoral program had a modest number of graduates, and was accredited by state and regional accrediting bodies. After the original faculty members and leadership ended their association, a new administration decided to concentrate on undergraduate programs, along with a few graduate degrees, but not the Ph.D., and established the Union Institute & University in Cincinnati, Ohio, unrelated to the University Without Walls program. The new structure pioneered distance learning, and opened centers in Florida and California in underserved areas. The experimental Ph.D. program disappeared leaving memories of some accomplished and significant people.

(3) In 1838, to save Georgetown University from financial ruin, the Jesuits sold more than 272 enslaved people, whom they referred to as "servants" from their five Maryland tobacco plantations. Some of these enslaved individuals;

women, men, children and even infants were torn from their families and sold to plantation owners in southern Louisiana. The story was lost to history until 2004 when it was uncovered by a descendent while researching her family tree. On September 20, 2019, the GU 272 Descendants Association and the president of the Jesuits Conference in the United States signed a memorandum of understanding (MOU) to establish a $1 billion irrevocable trust and a Descendants Truth & Reconciliation Foundation, which will work to address and heal the wounds of that betrayal of human dignity.

(4) The *Fordham Urban Law Journal* confers the Louis J. Lefkowitz Award annually upon an outstanding individual who has improved the quality of life in New York City.

Chapter 2

The Viking

It was A dinner at the NYU Club in Manhattan prior to a concert. The club was located on the third floor of the historic Town Hall, at 123 West 43rd Street. Town Hall was founded by a group of suffragists in 1921, and designed by America's premier architects, McKim, Mead and White. The NYU Club offered dinner and theater packages for its members who were alumni, faculty and staff of the university. I was dining with my first wife, Natalie, who was staring at someone or something across the formal dining room. She said, "See that woman, in the black dress at the table in the corner?" I acknowledged I did. "Well," Natalie continued I went to summer camp with her over fifteen years ago."

I looked closer at the woman and her dining companion. "Well," I said. "I went to high school and college with the man she's with, and his name is Bob." And indeed, I had. I had grown up in Long Beach, New York a seacoast community, on a small island, accessed by a bridge from Long Island. There was one high school, therefore everyone at least recognized everyone else. I knew Bob, but he didn't know me. Bob's family was well off and their home, a Mediterranean style villa was across the road from the great bay between Long Beach and the mainland. The family owned a major television rating company. Bob was a burley guy, just about six feet tall, and not at all handsome. But he was charming, and high school girls were attracted to his semi dangerous kind of bored manner. Bob began smoking cigarettes at age fourteen. He preferred Camels, unfiltered of course, the industry's strongest. At the time, Camels were marketed everywhere with the slogan, "More doctors smoke Camels than any other cigarette."

Bob, graduated from Long Beach High School two years prior to my graduating. I began as a freshman at Boston University, where Bob was a junior. I had graduated from high school at age sixteen and was unsophisticated, and no doubt, boring. So Bob didn't know me. At BU, we rushed fraternities our first semester, probably a really bad idea. I joined Phi Alpha the "nice guys" Jewish fraternity at the university. Bob, had been recruited by Phi Epsilon Pi the "wealthy cool guys" Jewish fraternity. The fraternity houses were actually in different towns, mine in Alston and Bob's in Brookline. Therefore, Bob and I rarely ran into each other over our time at BU. I left Boston after my junior year, for financial reasons, and graduated from NYU where I stayed on for graduate school. Bob graduated and we didn't see each other until nine years later at the NYU Club.

This time Bob was gracious and welcoming to me. Our new families were similar in composition. We both had two children, a boy and a girl, and the girl was the older sibling. Bob's kids were several years older than ours, but we had many good times together as families. Bob, and his family resided in Queens County in the Hillcrest community near Utopia Parkway, in a pleasant single-family home. The Utopia Parkway area was originally intended as a haven for Jewish Immigrants living in crowed and unsanitary conditions on Manhattan's Lower East Side. In 1905, fifty acres of land were purchased for the planned "Utopia," which regretfully was never developed, and then abandoned in 1935.

That was, of course especially interesting to me. Only the name Utopia Parkway survived the noble intentions.

We lived in North Tarrytown, in Westchester County, also in a single-family home. Bob, was an insurance broker selling casualty insurance to residential and commercial clients, and later became a general agent for the Guardian Life Insurance Company. Former major leaguer Joe Garagiola was one of Bob's celebrity clients. Garagiola had played baseball for the Cards, Pirates, Cubs and NY Giants, and then spent a decade as a regular on NBC's morning program, *The Today Show*. Through Joe Garagiola's sports and entertainment industry contacts, Bob's agency became the place for insurance among a certain stratum of New Yorkers. Among his clients was a good representation of New York area physicians. Medicare, had only just begun in 1967, so "Park Avenue" doctors had not felt the need to join the national health insurance program for people over sixty five.

Private insurance such as Blue Shield contracted with the member, not with the provider. Therefore, physicians charged, and were paid whatever the medical practice could command. Therefore, it was not unusual for New York City doctors to earn in the high six figures, or even more. Bob prospered from his association with sports and medical clients, which was not surprising since Bob could sell almost anything to anyone.

Bob's son from the time he was a young child, had serious trouble sleeping due to a respiratory issue that was difficult to diagnose. After seeing many doctors and some hospital stays, the boy was diagnosed as having cystic fibrosis, which at the time was an almost certain fatal disease. Bob tried coping with the realization that his son's future was limited, and for several years acted like any rational father whose child's health was fragile and unpredictable. Happily, his son finished high school, and graduated from college, and married. He moved to California where the family business was located. All of his son's great progress should have made Bob happy, but it didn't, as he confided in me one day. We had become close friends and were regularly in touch. Our children were adults, and Bob had moved to another insurance company, and gained more celebrities as clients. He said, "Ron, I can't pretend any longer. I'm scared about my son. He's at the outward edge of survival for his illness. That's all I think about. I'm changing my life. I'm becoming a Viking." It wasn't possible to be more surprised. I asked, "Viking, is that a thing?" Bob answered quietly, "No, but Vikings didn't answer to anyone. They went where they wanted to go, and no one dared to stop them." I reminded Bob that Vikings wandered the earth a thousand years ago, when most of the earth was uninhabited, so there were few complaints about Vikings' robbing and pillaging.

We actually had another connection that we didn't realize, until years later. Long Beach was a summer resort. At every beach entrance was a small wood structure that housed the collection agent for beach passes and fees from visitors. The collection agent at the Grand Boulevard beach was my grandfather, Mike Roth. It was a good summer job for a senior, and coveted by many. Grandpa Mike, knew everyone important in our town so he held the job for many years. Stationed at each beach entrance was a Good Humor ice cream man with a bicycle propelled freezer. For three summers, while he was in college the Good Humor man who became a good friend of my grandfather was Bob. We discovered this one time during our afternoon phone calls. I still remember his surprised comment, "Mr. Roth was your grandfather? I loved him."

Bob and I, and millions of other Americans were experiencing a permanent change in the culture and structure of the society in which we had been raised. The time in the 1980s, perhaps the most significant period between the end of World War II, and the launching of Facebook in 2004, was poised to initiate unimagined social change in America. The internet's official beginning was in 1983. The personal computer, developed in the 1970s, began to show up on desks in business, and government offices in the 1980s. The first models that were manufactured by a variety of companies, from the mighty IBM down to Commodore, a former typewriter repair company, were even being purchased for use at home. The early PCs were difficult to operate, required some knowledge of programming, had limited capacity, and were expensive.

The 1980's also saw for the first time a significant reduction in smokers, which began in the late 1970s, with the outlawing of distributing free cigarettes. At the time smoking was permitted almost everywhere. Even in hospitals, with oxygen in use for patients with breathing problems. It appeared that everyone was smoking cigarettes. On television, smoking was everywhere as it had been in movies for decades. Finally in the 1970's actual scientific research, not the kind done by cigarette companies, proved without any doubt that smoking contributed to diseases and death of smokers. There was even a hint of future research that would prove that something called, "second hand smoke," was also dangerous. However, it took twenty years for the United States Government to get solidly behind the move to stop Americans from smoking. Southern senators, from tobacco producing states, successfully blocked government "interference" with the cigarette manufacturers. Many people, in and outside of government, believed that it was not the proper role of federal government to tell citizens to stop smoking, similar to the present-day anti-vaccination freaks, who would rather die than be told to do something healthy by the government.

The actor Ronald Reagan, was elected president in 1980 as the protector of the rich and powerful. Reagan, stupid, sleepy and incompetent proclaimed, "The government is the problem," setting the agenda of the Republican Party to this very time, which pretends it desires a smaller government, while aching for an authoritarian government, led by the lifelong failure at anything resembling a human being, Donald Trump. Reagan, as president during the 1980s, shifted the thinking of many Americans away from caring for their fellow citizens. Governor Mario Cuomo, of New York, summed up Reagan when he said, "Ronald Reagan made the denial of compassion acceptable."

The cellular phone was introduced in 1983. Mobile phones of various sizes, and capacity had been available for twenty years. However, the smaller cell phone, we all began to depend on, was an innovation that changed lives and fortunes almost instantly. The use of cell phones grew quickly, and in the early 1990's, smart phones were introduced for taking pictures and videos, giving directions while driving, calculations, note taking, exchanging cash, internet access, texting and even talking to each other. Carrying a smart phone has become more important than carrying your wallet. However, the most unlikely cultural event that could be imagined by a Viking in the 1980's, or by anyone else at the time, would be the soon to be ubiquitous on-line matchmaking and dating.

Bob and I had lots of lively talks regarding his view of life, during the following year. Mostly Bob would call in the late afternoon, when I was in my college office finishing up a grant proposal or preparing for my evening class, in technical writing. It was a graduate level course required for nurse educators and taken by teachers as well. The nurses were relentless, and some would remind me that they had not ever gotten a grade other than an A. Bob, on the other hand, was becoming more depressed and one afternoon, he revealed that his marriage was over. That surprised me, although the last time he showed up at our home in Westchester for a New Year's Day brunch, he was alone, and driving a new black low-slung sports-type car that I couldn't identify and forgot to ask about. "Yeah, well, my affair was discovered so it was a good time to leave." I was surprised and said so. Bob told me his lover's name, which I recognized from our time at Boston University. "Bob, is she still married? Her husband was a Phi Ep, one of your fraternity brothers." He acknowledged that it was true. "We saw each other every Wednesday for years at a hotel in Little Neck. But one day as we left the hotel we saw my wife sitting in her car watching us. I told her to go home and forget about it, which is what a Viking would do."

One week later, Bob called with a corollary to his last reveal. The affair, no longer secret, Bob and his lover decided to leave their respective marriages, and get away from New York for a while in order to make plans for a permanent relationship. They settled on the day, and Bob felt that his life as a Viking was about to begin. However, it was not to be. Two days before they were planning to leave the city his lover's college age son had an accident while skiing, and broke his leg in two places. He was home in bed and helpless, until the bones healed. His mom would not leave him even for the adventure of a lifetime with a Viking.

I always remained in touch with Bob, especially through phone calls in the late afternoon. My own marriage had ended and I was living on a college campus in North Yonkers. I'd visit Bob occasionally, in his apartment in Forest Hills, in the Queens section of New York City. One night after our dinner at Ben's Kosher Delicatessen Bob confided he had been seeing a woman, and believed he could have a loving relationship with her. Susan, was an interior designer, sophisticated, and in the midst of a messy awful divorce, from her physician husband. She feared that all of their money would be squandered by the expensive divorce lawyers they each had hired. Bob had advised her when there was absolutely nothing else that could be billed in behalf of either client the divorce would be completed, which worked out exactly that way. Susan had grown up in a life of luxury. Her father was a surgeon, and the president of Memorial Sloan Kettering in New York the most advanced hospital for the study and treatment of cancer in the world. Her family lived in the pent house on the hospital's roof, and Susan attended a private academy on Manhattan's Eastside. On weekends they would leave the city for their country estate in Dutchess County, NY, where there were horses for Susan to ride. Over the following two years we had good times with Bob and Susan. I had remarried, and even though Bob was still not divorced Susan remained in love with him.

Both Bob and my wife Kathleen, were good tennis players. Occasionally Bob would come to New Jersey for tennis with Kathleen, on the courts of the college where I was associated, which was only three miles from our home. It was a summer Saturday, and Bob came out and after lunch he and Kathleen went off to the campus. About two hours later they returned. While Bob was washing up, and changing his clothing, Kathleen appearing to be worried said, "There's something wrong with Bob. I beat him in every game we played." In deed there was something wrong with Bob. He had smoked cigarettes since a young teen, and recently had been warned by his doctor that the veins in his legs were collapsing causing havoc with his circulatory system. He had potential for stroke, heart attack, and a dozen other deadly issues. Would he curtail his smoking, no, not this Viking. However, a short time later Bob during one of our serious talks proclaimed, "I have no more hope and no more dreams." A serious and concerning statement spoken by a good friend. Two months later, while Bob's brother who was the head of the family business was attending a conference in Florida. Bob flew to Miami to see him. While they were in the hotel's elevator Bob collapsed and died.

Susan asked me to accompany her to Bob's funeral service held at the grave site in a cemetery on Long Island. When I showed up Bob's family members were smiling and pleased to see me, until they saw I was with Susan. For a long time, after he died, I was angry with Bob. I believed his crazy Viking persona prevented him from quitting smoking. I missed him. I missed our talks, and his great sense of humor. The dull afternoons were duller. And then one day, I had an epiphany. I realized that Bob really was a Viking. He gave up his life so he would not see his son become fatally ill.

CHAPTER 3

Why I Love Coffee

Growing up in Long Beach, New York, an island community connected by a bridge from Long Island, summer meant swimming every day, and fishing on Saturday. It was the 1950s when television was just getting started so boys living by the water fished. The town dock stretched far out into Reynolds Channel a great deep bay, and every Saturday my group of three friends and I met at 6:30 AM to fish for fluke with our bamboo rods equipped with Penn reels, and salt water lines before the power boats churned up the water. We shared a box of earth worms purchased at Pete's bait shop for a dollar, a significant cost at the time, considering egg creams and Devil Dogs cost a nickel apiece at Harry & Max's Sweet Shop.

Fluke are great flat fish sort of a cousin to the flounder, which our families enjoyed having for dinner Saturday nights. Along with the bait and a medium sinker we would hang a shiny lure that reflected light once in the water. The fluke would be attracted by the silver glow, and go after the bait. Our catch, which we shared often contained some fish that weighed over five pounds.

It was always cold on the water before dawn, and we never remembered to bring jackets so we shivered until the sun came up. But, around 7:30 my father would drive up to the pier in his black Packard automobile delivering cardboard containers of sweet and light coffee, known as "regular" in all of the luncheonettes and diners in New York, along with delicious prune Danish pastries, wrapped in waxed paper, from Hittelman's bakery, on Park Avenue the town's main street. My friends were ecstatic, and I was proud of my dad for his thoughtfulness, but that was just the way he was. I was an only child so my parents doted on me, and delivering coffee every summer Saturday morning to his son, and his son's friends was something my father enjoyed.

The fishing continued until we entered high school, and Saturdays took on other activities that included sports and sleeping late. The fishing group disbanded, and re-banded into other groups connected to teams, dating, school dances and working to save money to pay for college, which was actually possible to do in those days. We all remained friends, and would still get together on occasion to play penny ante poker on a Friday night, and talk about the girls who attended our high school. After the poker games we would head to the Rex Restaurant also on Park Avenue, a long narrow place that served up the newly introduced food sensation, pizza.

I realized, years later after graduating from college just how much the Saturday morning coffee and Danish run meant to my father. He was older than my friend's fathers actually forty one when I was born. By today's standards that's young, but not then. We didn't play ball or ride bikes as a family, so he participated in my life by supplying hot and sweet coffee to our group of adolescent fisherman, most summer Saturday mornings. What I didn't realize, was my family's dire financial situation. Unknown to me, was the bankruptcy of the business my father owned with his brothers, followed by my father's personal bankruptcy, which resulted in civil lawsuits, legal bills and a life style reversal. In the 1950s the culture was tell nothing, rather than tell all as it is today. So I wasn't aware of our shift in circumstances, which was purposely kept from me. My parents had to cut back on every expense, and in fact, we moved to a small house with the explanation that we didn't need all of the rooms in our big house. The one part of our life that my father wouldn't change however, was the coffee and Danish pastry tradition, which somehow continued uninterrupted over the summers.

While in high school, I continued to drink regular coffee every morning, but in college switched to having it black and still enjoy it that way. Sometimes while drinking the hot beverage on a cold day, I'm reminded of the early mornings on the fishing pier, and my father always showing up when we needed him the most. Our family that included my mother's parents moved from Tuckahoe, NY to Long Beach when I was about eight years old. We had lived in a large Spanish style house on Plymouth Avenue with sprawling lawns, and big shade trees. During World War II, my father had a large Victory Garden planted in the back of the property that was tended by a local man. My parents were not gardeners. Both had grown up in urban areas, my dad in Bayonne, New Jersey, and my mom in Los Angeles, California. One day two Mayflower moving vans appeared and packed up all of the furniture in the house. One van headed to Long Beach, the other to a storage facility. I didn't mind moving to Long Beach because I didn't have friends living in my neighborhood. Most of my school classmates, lived below the steep hills that bordered the west side of the Bronx River Parkway, and my school. My mother didn't drive, so when the school bus dropped me off every day, I was alone most of the time.

We moved into a rented brick Tudor style house on West Market Street. The house was one of eight identical homes, built in a row prior to the war. It was less than half of the size of our house in Tuckahoe, but was comfortable enough, and children around my age lived next door and down the street. We were always outside in the warm weather playing stoop ball, potsie, ringolvio, and at each other's home when it was too cold to be outside. The older boys played stick ball in the street, and we younger guys watched with envy dreaming of the day we would be old enough to play ball with pink Spaulding's, in the street. I loved the companionship. This continued through junior high and high school. We moved again a few years later to a bigger house a block away, and our furniture that had been in storage was delivered to us making my mother very happy.

My parents were Johanna Roth Kase, and Gustave Kase both born in 1899. My mother in Brooklyn and my father in Harlem. His family moved to Bayonne when he was a young teenager to join other family members in operating a grocery store. The store had a majority of Polish speaking customers so Gustave learned to speak Polish. He was also completely fluent in Castilian Spanish, learned while an honor student in Bayonne High School. One of my favorite memories of my father was the time my high school Spanish teacher Senorita Fulgado frustrated with my poor performance in her class insisted that my mother come to school to discuss my class participation. My mother was not the one to do that. So one afternoon, fresh from having commuted from Manhattan, my father dressed in a great dark suit, starched white shirt, and fine tie came to my high school. On the way to the Senorita's classroom, he spotted the principal and asked, "Joe, are you taking part in the meeting?" The principal, a great guy answered, "Not a chance." We entered the Spanish teacher's classroom, and before anything else happened my father greeted the Senorita in perfect Spanish, and they had a conversation. I didn't have an issue in my Spanish class ever again.

My mother's parents Amelia Henoch Roth, and father Michael Roth were also born in New York City. My grandmother in 1878 and grandfather in 1879. My grandmother's parents Jacob and Bertha Henoch, my great grandparents, emigrated from Prussia in 1860 a year before the U.S. Civil War began. They had lived peacefully in Cologne, before the unification of Germany. Even though Jews had lived in the region since Roman times, and were well integrated into the prevailing culture, the Henoch family embarked for America in the latter part of 1859 sensing there would always be a barrier between them, and other Germans. Also, they believed that America offered a chance for some prosperity. How they had learned anything about America at that time is still a mystery. They were working class like almost everyone else. Jacob blocked men's hats as his trade and Bertha was a competent seamstress.

Traveling the 200 miles from Cologne to the port of Bremen in 1859 wasn't an easy task. Most of the several week's long trip was by horse and wagon, which made Bertha ill, as she was pregnant, with their first child. The sea voyage provided no relief, and when they finally arrived in New York happily they found other German speaking Jewish immigrants who helped them settle in the city. They had brought with them some gold coins sewed into their clothing that they had acquired by saving every penny for three years. Unlike most of the others of, "The Great European Migration" that took place between 1800 and 1915, the Henoch's had enough funds to sustain them and open a tailor shop.

Jacob and Bertha, remained in Manhattan's lower East Side for the rest of their lives. They had eight children. My grandmother Amelia, known to me as Molly was their second youngest child born in 1878. In 1898, Amelia married Michael Roth always called Mike. Grandpa Mike, was my best friend when we lived in Tuckahoe. Each afternoon, he met me at the school bus stop. In the fall, we would steal apples from the trees near the bus stop. He showed me how to cut the apple's skin off in one long piece. He had wonderful surprises for me like fancy marbles and wood puzzles. I don't know anything about my grandfather's family roots in Europe. He didn't talk about it, and it didn't occur me to ask even though he lived until he was 93, and remained sharp until the end. My best guess is that Mike's parents emigrated from the Austrian territory known then as Galicia sometime in the 1870s. Galicia was a large area covering the present southwestern Poland, and western Ukraine.

Galicia in the mid-1800s was home to about a half million Jews known as Galitizianers who lived there without the rights of the Christian Russian Orthodox population. They spoke Yiddish, and worked as tradesmen, tailors, dentists, lawyers, and hat makers. The region was the place where Hasidism was begun and practiced. The beaver hat outfits still worn by Hasidic males are copies of the clothing worn by the Polish princes who controlled the region and persecuted Jewish residents. The Jews who did not emigrate prior to the mid-1930s were murdered by the occupying Germans with the assistance of Poles and Ukrainians. The author Henry Roth, *Call it Sleep, Shifting Landscape, Mercy of a Rude Stream,* was born in Tysmenitz, Galicia in 1906, and came to America with his parents in 1908. In photos taken late in his life Henry Roth looks remarkably like my grandfather Mike Roth.

My grandfather Mike, had been the prop manager for 20th Century Fox studios in Hollywood. His career began in Queens at the earliest movie studios where silent films were first produced. Then he moved to Fort Lee, New Jersey, which had become the center for all movie making in the United States. However, California's great weather, large open spaces, desert backgrounds and available horses for the popular Western movies, were attracting studio executives to a place known as Hollywood. The Roth family, now including my mother and her younger brother Sidney moved to Los Angles, and rented a large white stucco house, in the Wilshire section of the city. Mike was good at finding locations especially for Western movies, renting the horses, buying the furnishings, renting the cars and wagons, and anything else needed to make a movie. We have two large Fu dogs, ceramic pieces in our dining room, acquired as props by my grandfather, for a silent movie made in the 1920s featuring, Anna May Wong the first Asian-American actress in a Hollywood film.

Life in California was happy for the Roth's. They visited Catalina Island often and enjoyed California life, and the mild weather during the early part of the 20th Century until the 1930s. Mike's good friends, and poker buddies, were cowboy movie stars, Tom Mix, Hoot Gibson and Will Rogers. As the motion picture business matured new younger people were taking control of the studios that had slowly converted from silent films to talkies. By this time my mother had left Los Angles and moved to New York since prospects for marriage were few. Hannah was a flapper and attractive, but didn't have a serious relationship so she decided to join some friends who had left Los Angeles, and now resided in New York City. Her brother Sidney followed her two years later, and after another year, Mike frustrated with the new Hollywood studio executives, and the industry's conversion to talking movies moved with Molly to New York as well.

At the time, all of the financial business of movie making was conducted in New York City. Through one of Mike's contacts, my mother started a job at MGM's main office in mid-town Manhattan. She stayed for five years making wonderful friendships with women who remained her friends for the rest of her life. My parents met in 1936, and married after a few months, and lived on the Grand Concourse in the Bronx, in an art nouveau apartment building. When I was born two years later, they bought the Spanish style house in Tuckahoe, NY, and my grandparents Mike and Molly Roth moved in with us occupying the former servants' section of the house that included a living and dining area, bedroom and bathroom, and a separate stairs to the kitchen. It worked out perfectly as they had privacy when needed, and we did as well.

My father, had been married previously, and he and wife Frances had a daughter they named Marsha. I saw my half-sister only a few times in our lives. The last was when I attended the annual conference of high school newspaper editors at Columbia University. The two-day yearly event attracted hundreds of high schoolers. I stayed in the city with my parents at my Uncle Kermit's luxury apartment, on Central Park South, and Marsha with husband Bill Forest a local radio personality showed up. Relations between Marsha and our father had been strained for several years due to on-going legal issues from the twenty-five year old divorce. However, we had a nice time that evening. Marsha, had an attractive appearance with a dark complexion like our father. Regretfully, I never saw her again. Strangely we learned from a story in the New York *Daily News,* several years later, that Bill Forest had died while in Japan after eating improperly cut and cooked blowfish. Recently through Ancestry, I found that Marsha had married again and had lived on Long Island.

My father's family story is quite different. His parents Soel Kase and Pearl Berknoff were also born in Galicia then a part of the Austria-Hungary Empire. Their immigration information indicates they were from Austria, but it's doubtful that either had ever actually been to Austria itself, and certainly not Vienna. They met after immigrating to America. Soel, in about 1880 and Pearl, in 1884. They met in New York, married and had six children. My father was the second youngest. Pearl, perhaps traveling alone, or perhaps not from the outreaches of Eastern Europe to

America, wound her way to Spain, and then Lisbon, in Portugal. Pearl, booked passage on the steamship *Adriatic* owned by the I.C. Collins Shipping Company, which sailed from Lisbon to Rio de Janeiro, Brazil. Jewish refugees from Eastern Europe were found in Brazil, Bolivia, Argentina, Colombia and Ecuador at that time. Some stayed, and established families and businesses that still exist today. I don't know how long Pearl stayed in Rio de Janeiro, and if she was alone there or with friends or family members, but eventually, it appears, she boarded one of the Lamport & Holt Line steamships bound for New York.

I didn't know my grandmother Pearl, but did know grandpa Soel who always dressed well and looked prosperous. After Pearl passed away, Soel decided to live in an upscale place in Morristown, NJ, called *Aurora,* which today would be referred to as an assisted living complex. His sons happily paid all of the expenses, since they were all doing well in their respective businesses. Soel always said he was the poorest resident of *Aurora* because it was filled with old ladies from wealthy families.

My father, mother, and I were close. They were always supportive of everything I tried on my way to adulthood. My father attended the University of Pennsylvania, for one year. He was unable to continue paying for tuition and living expenses so he had to drop out. He completed his education at Pace College, on Park Row, in Manhattan where he earned a degree in accounting. In 1983 he was awarded the Pace University Gold Medal, for Outstanding Alumni.

My father, and two of his brothers owned a company called, Glida Corporation of America. The company's office was in the Empire State Building, and their factories were located in Binghamton, NY. The Glida Corporation was one of the original tenants of the new Empire State Building on Manhattan's 5th Avenue and 34th Street. The president of the Empire State Building Company was Alfred E. Smith the former governor and presidential candidate who would have a friendly greeting for my father whenever they saw each other in the building's lobby. Hanging in Glida's outer office was an oil painting of Franklin Delano Roosevelt painted by John Howard Sanden.

Glida, manufactured a large variety of household and baby care products sold in every department store chain in the nation. A subsidiary Kase Rubber Company that operated mostly in England pioneered the rubber covering of fabric to make it water proof prior to the introduction of vinyl. The company patterned a slide fastener the *Glida* that closed cloth bags used for holding cosmetics, and other travel items. Also, Glida was a contractor for the U.S. Army manufacturing all manner of equipment for solders. However, after decades of success the Glida Corporation was unable to maintain its edge in the consumer market, and new products from competitors sold to a new generation of store buyers ended the company's dominant position in the market place. Glida, declared bankruptcy in 1960, and ceased operations a year later.

I left Long Beach for college, and never really returned to live there. I married at twenty, and moved to Riverdale in the West Bronx. We had two wonderful children, Betsy and Kenneth who made my parent's life complete. Nothing else gave them the joy as being with my children, which they regularly experienced. After a few years, my parents followed us to Riverdale, and then moved to White Plains, NY. They stayed there for the rest of their lives. My father died at age 92 and my mother at 97. One day, toward the end of my father's life I told him that he was a great father. He replied, "You're a better one."

On the following page is the original U.S. patent material for the slide fastener, called "Glida."

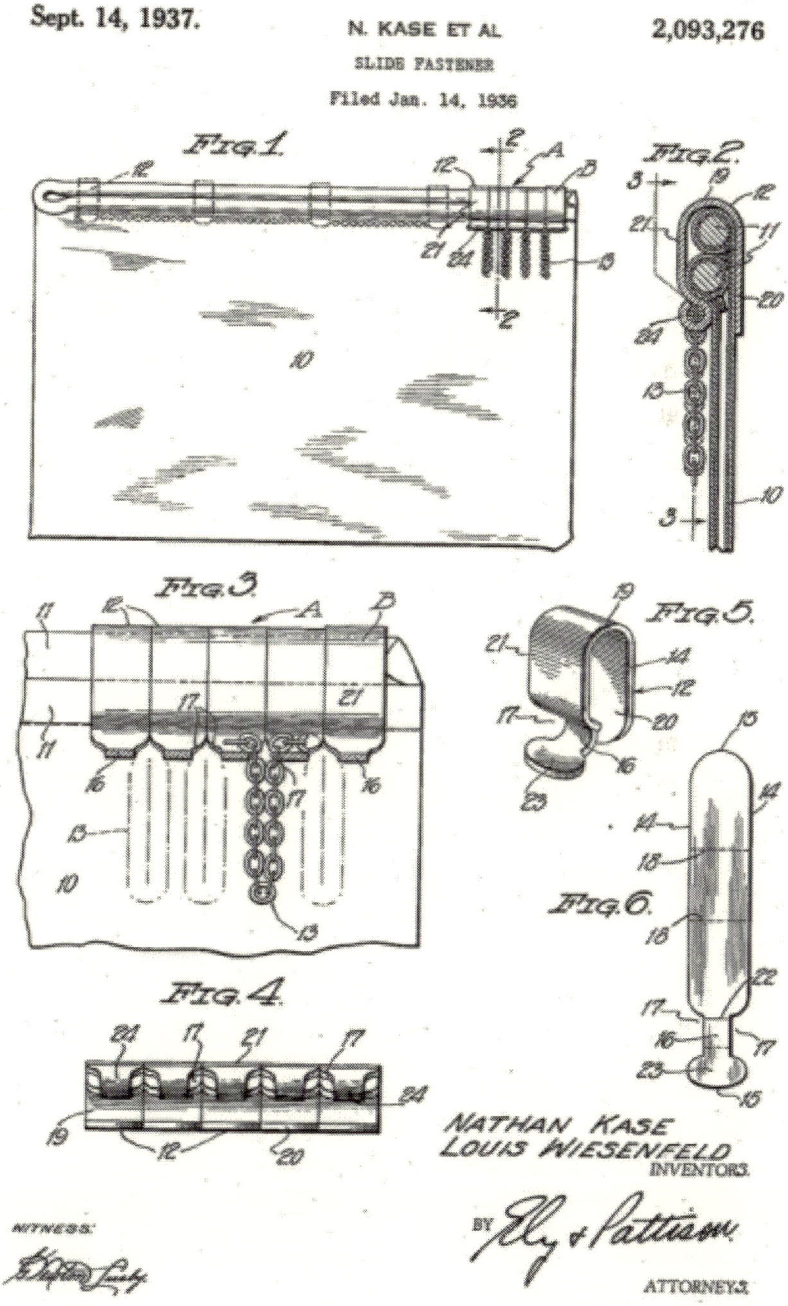

Sept. 14, 1937.
N. KASE ET AL
2,093,276
SLIDE FASTENER
Filed Jan. 14, 1936
FIG. 1.
FIG. 2.
FIG. 3.
FIG. 4.
FIG. 5.
FIG. 6.
NATHAN KASE
LOUIS WIESENFELD
INVENTORS.
WITNESS:
BY
ATTORNEYS.

Chapter 4

The Jewish Atheist Who Enjoys Christmas

CHRISTMAS, IS A state of being to me, and probably is different to almost everyone who celebrates that exceptional time of the year. I feel no faith, or belief in Christmas as a spiritual event, but I enjoy the entire season as it rolls out cumulating in a day of family happily being together, and always enjoying our delicious roasted turkey, my own recipe stuffing, and Kathleen's vegetables, gravy, deserts, and who knows what else. From the time the lights begin to appear on trees and houses to mark the holiday's beginning, I look forward to more decorations, on the streets I frequent. The Christmas season is important to retail business, and that's okay. It means that more people are employed to help with the increase of purchasing because almost everyone, believer, atheist, and different religion observer, somehow becomes imbued with at least some of the culture that encourages polite exchanges among us. Others, just want to be as friendly and happy as they possibly can be, and that's good because the rest of the year can be tense and unhappy due to the multi complexity, of our high tech, politically upset society. Therefore, we need Christmas to pause our endeavors, and shop for presents, and buy too much food, and especially acknowledge the people who make our lives, good and happy.

Our home like the Graham Nash song, *Our House*, is a very fine house. I have enjoyed living here with Kathleen and Jonathan for all the years we have been married. The house was built in the 1870s in the style called, "American Four Square." The four outside walls were delivered flat probably by horse and wagon, and carpenters put the structure together, finishing the interior in the traditional manner. We have renovated the entire house during three projects, which have expanded both floors. Unfortunately, the original lemonade porch disappeared sometime during the last century and a simpler set of steps, and small porch was added. Albert Einstein's home in Princeton, NJ, was an American Four Square, and an exact duplicate of our original house.

About fifteen years ago we added a garage built by a great Amish company from Pennsylvania. The elements of the garage arrived, on a flatbed truck similar to our original American Four Square house. It was accompanied by three young men, who were excellent carpenters. The garage was never intended to house cars. Instead the ground floor became Jonathan's pool hall, and the second that had a ping pong table for a while became a hangout for watching the games for Jonathan and his friends. In fact, Jonathan's "Garage Parties" became famous locally, and he hosted up to sixty guests at the Thanksgiving Eve get togethers, New Year's Eve and other celebrations for many years. One summer, while we were in Copenhagen we discovered the Garage Parties were a topic discussed even there by local young people, due to one Danish exchange student who had attended some of them.

Our house, at Christmas glows with Kathleen's great sense of décor, as she fills our place with decorations acquired over the decades, we have been together. After New Year's Day the decorations remain, and are slowly, really slowly removed over the following two months. I think it's great that Christmas doesn't suddenly finish according to a date on the calendar, but its spirit remains for as long as possible. And invariably for at least a month, Kathleen finds presents she had wrapped, but forgot to label for Jonathan and me, so the gift giving continues for a while. Also included in the spirit and calendar of the Christmas season is Chanukah, which we have at times lit candles, in a menorah for eight days when Jonathan was in elementary school. While he was in kindergarten, Jonathan was considered exotic since he was the only child in his class with some kind of Jewish connection, as mild as ours actually was. Therefore, when Chanukah came up Kathleen, my Irish-Catholic wife, was asked by the teacher to lead the Chanukah celebration in Jonathan's school, which she did perfectly. For all of these reasons, the Jewish atheist enjoys Christmas.

Religion has never been a part of my life, and I believe I'm better for it. I'm proud to be Jewish however, because I believe the Jewish people have made great contributions that have advanced human kind, and have done a minimal amount of damage. I have helped anyone who has come to me with needs that I can possibly assist with. I do it because, it's the right thing to do, and not because I will be rewarded in any manner. My reward is my wife Kathleen, my children, Betsy, Kenneth and Jonathan, and Jonah my grandson, who are good and charitable people. My parents were atheists, Jewish atheists. They didn't believe there was a supreme being running the lives of billions of people around the world. That just didn't make any sense to either of them, and it was informally passed on to me. However, when I was twelve my mother decided I should become a bar mitzvah, since every other boy I knew, in our Long Beach community was going in that direction, and we were very much culturally Jewish. It was our ethnicity.

I was registered, in the afternoon Hebrew school of Temple Beth-El, a conservative synagogue located a few blocks from our home, on Lindell Boulevard in Long Beach. There was a reformed temple in the East End Section of Long Beach, but it was too far to walk to and from, and my mother didn't drive. The Hebrew teacher was Mr. Besdene, and even then I worried about how he could possibly earn enough money to support his family. He was nice enough, but I hated trying to learn Hebrew, and especially disliked the stories from the bible that our class had to endure on Sundays. The stories just didn't make any sense, and I wanted to know who wrote them, and why were they important enough to bother twelve year olds, with their often unpleasant messages such as turning a man's wife into a pillar of salt? One day, out of pure frustration with me, Mr. Besdene, called my home and spoke with my mother. His message was, "Mrs. Kase, your son will never be a rabbi." My mother responded, "Thank god."

CHAPTER 5

Neil O'Connell, OFM

HOW CAN BEST friends, close friends, be so different in one major aspect of life, that it's unimaginable that their friendship would endure for thirty-five years? Yet it did, and I will always be grateful for the time spent with NEIL O'CONNELL. Neil was only a year older than me, and was in the last stages of Parkinson's disease when I first began to write about him. We had not seen each other since the beginning of the Covid-19 pandemic, which began almost four years ago. We were no longer able to speak on the telephone because Neil wasn't able to communicate verbally any longer. For about two years, I regularly sent letters with photos and announcements, and packages of treats to Neil who had been residing in the St. Elizabeth's Mother House, a home and an infirmary for the Franciscan Sisters of Allegany, an order of Catholic nuns, located about an hour south of Buffalo, NY.

Neil had received wonderful loving care at St. Elizabeth's, since he moved to upstate New York, five years ago from St. Petersburgh, Florida. The leadership of the Franciscan Sisters of Allegany decided to begin accepting priests of the Franciscan order who required long term care. Neil was the first. Neil O'Connell, is a Catholic priest and a Franciscan of the Order of Franciscans Minor (OFM). He was also in great need for daily care due to the ravages of Parkinson's. Neil had resided in a friary, a beautifully renovated former three story hotel, in downtown St. Petersburgh, Florida. The center is owned by the Franciscan order, and is a retirement home for their members. Kathleen and I visited Neil there in 2019, and realized that he had lost a great deal of physical strength. We spent two days with Neil, and knew he was suffering, but not complaining. We were relieved when he called a few weeks later, to provide his new address in Allegany, NY.

Neil, is a tall man, over six feet, and a giant intellectually. He is a native and booster of Buffalo, NY, and attended public schools, until going to a Franciscan high school. Neil's mother was a public school teacher, and his father a captain in the Buffalo Fire Department. He had one brother a physician, who died in his early fifties. Neil, attended St. Bonaventure University in Allegany, NY for his undergraduate degree, and then a Catholic seminary for his ordination as a Franciscan priest. Later he attended Siena College located near Albany, NY for a master's degree, and the University of Georgia for his Ph.D. in British Tudor History, and then Catholic University, where he earned an additional doctorate in Sacred Theology. Obviously he was always busy. While at Georgia, Neil was also the Catholic chaplain. Later, when, on occasion, he would visit the University of Georgia in Athens, my son Kenneth a resident of Athens would meet up with him for dinner and good conversation. So how did Neil, a faithful Christian, a brilliant scholar and the most ethical person I have ever known, become my closest friend for so many years, well it's an interesting story.

From 1984 to 1988, I was the academic dean of a Catholic college in Yonkers, NY, with a small campus as well in Manhattan. Elizabeth Seton College was located on Broadway in North Yonkers, on a beautiful campus high above the Hudson River. What had begun forty years before as an academy for Catholic girls, many from prominent South American families was now a college struggling to survive. Half of the faculty members were Sisters of Charity, a Catholic order founded by Elizabeth Ann Seton in 1809. Even prior to Vatican II, which allowed Catholic nuns to abandon their black habits with stiff white cowls around their faces the Charities wore black bonnets and comfortable black dresses as had Elizabeth Seton, while mourning her late husband who died while they were in Italy. There are many other Sisters of Charity orders that are not related to the Seton Charity's. The college's president SISTER MARY ELLEN BROSNIN, and I were close colleagues, which was remarkable, since I was the only non-Catholic member of the college's executive committee. Often we would speak on the telephone at night after she left her office, and had her dinner. The college's financial condition was terrible, and additional funds were needed for repairs and maintenance of the campus' buildings that were showing extreme wear. We decided that I would leave the dean's position and become the vice president for institutional advancement, and grant seeker, in order to bring in needed external support, which had a good result. Therefore, we went about advertising for a new academic dean.

I was a member of the four person search committee, which read the cover letters and resumes of applicants answering the ad in *The New York Times* Sunday Education section. We interviewed three or four people, and then an applicant from Buffalo, who was the dean of the downtown City campus of Erie Community College a member of the SUNY system. Of course, the applicant was Neil O'Connell and his presence, his intellect, and his charming manner, captivated the search committee's members. It was the 1980s so everything relating to employment was done in person. The committee members agreed that

Neil would be scheduled to be interviewed by Sister Mary Ellen that afternoon.

I invited Neil to lunch with me in a restaurant in the next village Hastings-on-Hudson. We were immediately comfortable with each other. I asked the question, the other committee members missed, "Are you an active Catholic priest?" That was obvious to me after reading Neil's resume, but the committee members, all Catholics missed it. Neil was wearing a dark gray suit, white shirt and blue tie not the usual uniform of a Catholic priest. Neil confirmed he was a priest, and since his ordination had worked in higher education rather than in a parish. Also, he desired to live near Manhattan where the Franciscan friary is located. He explained that Franciscans usually wore traditional robes rather than the black suit with Roman collar, and that their mission was social justice, especially for the poor with which I certainly identified.

Upon returning to campus, I prepared Mary Ellen for her interview with Neil. Her reaction was unexpected. "I will not have a priest always looking over my shoulder. I leave that to you," she exclaimed. I assured her that Neil didn't want to second guess her leadership, and that he would bring a great amount of intellectualism and experience to the campus as well as social justice leadership, and would accept the low salary we offered. She asked, "How do you know all of that? You just met him."

Yes, that was true, but that day, Neil O'Connell and I forged the beginning of a friendship based on concern for anyone in need, and how to help those who are unable to enjoy progressing on their own. Mary Ellen gave in, and hired Neil, and they too, became great friends. Neil stayed at Seton College for a little while after I left there in 1988. It had become obvious that the college could not survive much longer, and I had begun to negotiate a takeover by Mercy College now a university, which was located on the Hudson River two villages north in Dobbs Ferry. I had taught as an adjunct in sociology at Mercy for almost ten years, and knew the members of the administration. Mercy College had grown dramatically, and had branch campuses in Yonkers, Yorktown Heights and the Bronx. What Mercy didn't have were residence halls, and Seton did. However, Mercy College was no longer controlled by a Catholic order of nuns. Its president and board of trustees were all lay people, and probably not all Catholics, so when I informed Mary Ellen of Mercy's interest in the campus, she refused to consider it. "It's not a Catholic college anymore," she wailed. "I have an agreement with Iona College in New Rochelle, and if they take the campus they will keep the Seton name."

I was dispatched to New Rochelle to work out the details of the merger of two colleges before it was ready to present to lawyers and trustees. Iona College is operated by the Irish Christian Brothers, a slippery group of guys I soon learned not to trust. A year after I left Seton's administration, I actually lived on its campus for two years, while going through a divorce. Iona acquired the campus and its assets. I had stayed in close touch with Mary Ellen, and actually had kept advising her to sell the property to a developer, and secure the future of the dozen Sisters of Charity living on campus, making meals communally and taking care of the stray cats that found their way there. Neil was unhappy with the proposed Seton/Iona partnership, but couldn't convince, Mary Ellen, that it was a mistake.

Neil, began his college teaching career at Prairie View A & M University, in Prairie View, Texas, an Historically Black University. After one year he applied to Fisk University, in Memphis, Tennessee. He was accepted as an associate professor and for eight years Neil taught European and British history at Fisk becoming department chairman, and Director of Humanities and Fine Arts. At the same time, he was chaplain for Catholic medical students at Meharry Medical College located close by to Fisk. Both institutions are also Historically Black Universities (HBCU). He performed countless marriages for Fisk and Meharry graduates, and then baptisms and family funerals. In addition to teaching at HBCU institutions, and as a recipient of the Ph.D. from the University of Georgia, Neil had experienced and understood the African American's delicate role not only in the South, but in the general American society. He, similar to Leo McLaughlin was comfortable at the Historically Black Universities, and spoke lovingly about the experience. Early in his profession to the Franciscans, Neil made an additional commitment, to always work to improve educational opportunities for African Americans.

Neil's parents had retired, and of course, were growing old so he petitioned to return to his beloved Buffalo, NY, and was offered a professorship, and the deanship of Erie Community College's City campus. He resided at a Franciscan friary in Buffalo, and saw his parents regularly, as well as his brother's large family who brought Neil into their circle of relationships and friends. He renewed the friendships from childhood, since people born there rarely leave Buffalo for long. After Neil's father passed away, his mom moved into an assisted living complex where many of her friends were residing so Neil felt comfortable to leave Buffalo once more, and join the administration of Seton College.

Seton College was located on the grounds of the William Boyce Thompson estate. The property had rolling hills, and was two hundred feet above the Hudson River. Thompson was a major industrialist in the field of mining copper all over the western United States, Canada and Peru. He financed lead, zinc and coal mines, street railways, steel producers, and silver mining, and controlled the Indian Motorcycle

Company, Cuba Cane Sugar Company, and Pearce-Arrow Motor Car Company among dozens of other companies which he financed.

Boyce Thompson as he was known, was born in 1869 in Montana, in the rough mining culture of the period. However, he attended, Phillips Exeter Academy in New Hampshire, and graduated from the Columbia School of Mines the predecessor of the College of Engineering of Columbia University. It's unclear how or why Boyce Thompson, in 1912 built Alder Manor in Yonkers, NY.

Just across from his estate on Route 9, the main north and south road at the time, he also built a three story rectangular building that became known as the Boyce Thompson Institute for Plant Research, which moved its operations to Ithaca, NY, in the 1980s, and is an internationally recognized center for research, and education. Alder Manor was designed by the famed architectural firm Carre and Hastings the architects who designed the main New York City Library on 5th Avenue, with the two gigantic lions guarding its entrance.

Thompson commissioned a ship and crew in 1910 to sail to Italy and Greece. His agents bought up statuary, paintings, garden pieces, and lots of furniture, tapestries, and the front of a three story Italian church, which was built into one side of Alder Manor. An indoor swimming pool was installed on the building's second floor over the kitchen. Each room was elegant, large and bright. The movie, "Crocodile Dundee" was partly filmed in Alder Manor, on the Seton College campus. Strangely Boyce Thompson never resided in Alder Manor, but lived in a more modest home in another part of Yonkers where he died in 1930, from pneumonia at age 61.The Sisters of Charity acquired the property in 1940 to establish a high school level academy for young women with a loan from the Catholic Archdiocese of New York. The loan was guaranteed by Sister Mary Ellen's father John Brosnin a partner in the law firm Mudge Rose Guthrie and Alexander, which later added Richard Nixon, and John Mitchell to its partnership. Thompson is buried in Sleepy Hollow Cemetery near Tarrytown, NY, known as the Headless Horseman region, because of Washington Irving's fable.

The college constructed a modern classroom building with wings for art classes, an auditorium, and a large gymnasium. A six story residence hall was added as well as two smaller halls for student living. Alder Manor was used for additional classes and seminars, celebrations and fund-raising events, and the former servant's wing became the living space for the Sisters of Charity. An additional building closer to the Hudson River that also housed the sisters was acquired. Alder Manor remained filled with the treasures brought back from Europe in 1910. During the entire Seton College era the walls were covered with painting by the old masters, Ming dynasty urns almost five feet tall stood in random places. It was considered rude to suggest the sale of the fine art and pottery, but I tried, and enlisted Neil in my quest to save the college. We contacted Christie's the famous art auction house in Manhattan. Mary Ellen had some kind of a relationship with Christie's so we believed it had a chance to work out. A Mr. Kelly, from the auction house arrived on campus one morning, and after a tour of the Manor's art collection Mary Ellen, and our art professor met with him, in the rose wood breakfast room. I was not involved. In those days so many smoked, and a bowl was set on the table as an ash tray. Mr. Kelly, expressed an interest in the ash covered bowl. He picked it up, and went into the adjacent kitchen, and washed and dried the bowl. Upon returning to the breakfast room he calmly informed Mary Ellen, and the art professor that the object was a Medici bowl possibly 600 years old, and priceless. However, nothing of the Boyce Thompson collection was ever sold by the sisters.

One spring morning in 1990 the telephone rang, at our house and a voice said, "Dr. Kase this is the president of St. Bonaventure University." I was startled and curious. Then I heard, "Ron its Neil. I was appointed president of St. Bonaventure, and I want to talk with you about it. St. Bonaventure University was controlled by the Franciscan order, and was seeking a new president so Neil was appointed to lead the institution during the time of declining college enrollment, and a financial crisis, which had frozen faculty salaries for several years. He was enthusiastic as always regarding new challenges. I attended his installation ceremony, which was appropriately Franciscan in nature. There were welcoming speeches from the chairman of the board of trustees, the faculty speaker, a student representative and the local congressman. Neil was eloquent and funny with his speech. Later dinner was served in the giant field house buffet style with Neil circulating, and finally sitting with me, Mary Ellen, and a few other friends. The change from over-the-top pomp and circumstances, and an expensive catered formal dinner for the inauguration of a college president was welcomed by all of us in the higher education field. St. Bonaventure University is situated on a flat valley plain with mountains as a back-drop. It's a beautiful place with matching buildings, and elegant lawns and landscaping. Neil stayed at St. Bonaventure for four years, and then he was called back to New York City to become the pastor of St. Stephen of Hungary RC Church, on East 82nd Street, in Manhattan.

It was Neil's first assignment to a church, and he immediately rose to the challenge of not only spiritual leadership, but the responsibility of every aspect of a busy parish. The first time I visited Neil at St. Stephen, I noticed that the Metropolitan Museum of Art, was only a few blocks west on 82nd Street. Neil was a devoted culture vulture, so I laughingly accused him of being at St Stephen because he could easily walk to the

Met whenever he wanted to. He didn't deny it. Neal, was a generous presenter of beautiful gifts for special occasions, mostly purchased at the Met's gift shop. We prize the set of candlesticks that Neil gave us when Jonathan was born, and the Passover plate he found for us while visiting Israel, as the guest of the Israeli government. Not content with his being the pastor of a church with a large active congregation that planned and held many community events, Neil who seemed to be on duty twenty-four hours a day, also taught in the history department of Marymount Manhattan College, on East 72nd Street, a fifteen minute walk from St. Stephen of Hungary.

While president of St. Bonaventure University, Neil, would come to our area for meetings with major donors. He was a masterful fund raiser or for events at the Franciscan friary. Sometimes he stayed with us if he didn't have to be in the city. Once when Notre Dame was playing Navy in football, in Giants Stadium in the Meadowlands, we bought tickets for the game. Our group of Kathleen and me, Neil, Kathleen's mom MARILYN FOLEY, our good friends KATHY MAHAFFEY, a professional photographer, and DAVID and JULIE KUBASKA. David was a beloved science teacher in the Eastchester, NY schools, and Julie was Vice President for Development at New York Medical College. We were enjoying the game, when a man sitting behind Neil asked where he had gotten the St. Bonaventure University jacket he was wearing. The man said his son was a student at the university, and he wanted to get him the same jacket. Neil said, "I'm president of St. Bonaventure, and I'll see that your son receives a jacket. He can come to my office when I'm back on campus." The man just snickered, "Yeah, thanks buddy, who you kidding?" and returned to the game. About fifteen minutes later, he asked again about the jacket. This time Neil had his business card ready, and handed it to the man behind him who read the name on the card and stammered, "Oh, Father, I'm so sorry." We all thought it was the game's highlight.

Eventually, Seton College, was given over to Iona College without any compensation to care for the sisters who lived on campus. Also, there were no provisions made for the preservation of the valuable art work housed in Alder Manor. The sisters were evicted in three months. The art and valuable objects were removed. Mary Ellen, was appointed to the position of assistant to the president of Iona College, and fired after one year. She later became ill, and lived out the rest of her life, a few more years in Mary the Queen, a nursing home for the sisters. The Seton campus was sold to the Yonkers Board of Education, which allowed the property to decay further. I visited the campus about two years ago with my son Kenneth. We drove around, but couldn't get close to Alder Manor, which was fenced off. The most striking change was the demolition of the large dormitory building that must have happened many years ago.

Recently I was pleased to learn that the Yonkers Board of Education had renovated the academic complex turning it into the William Boyce Thompson School, and changed the name of the entire campus to the Thompson Center. Happily Boyce Thompson has been remembered for his creation of a beautiful place. Sadly Elizabeth Seton College, has been forgotten.

After the presidency of St. Bonaventure University, and beginning as pastor of St. Stephen of Hungary, Neil, took some time to visit California, a place he hadn't been to before. Always staying with Franciscans, Neil, traveled frugally, but he enjoyed seeing new places. For several years, I brought groups of college students to London for three weeks in January. We stayed in Central London at Regents College, and the students took two courses and visited art museums, back stage of theaters and historic sites in and near London. In January of 1995, Neil came along to London with our study abroad group, and stayed at Regents College, and talked with the students regularly sharing his vast knowledge of British history. He had spent time in London many years previously doing research on Tudor England, for his doctoral thesis.

Just a month before we all left for London, Neil had officiated at the funeral of St. Bonaventure alumnus Thomas J. Mosser in Caldwell, NJ. Tom Mosser was the president of Burson-Marsteller, the world's largest public relations firm with branches throughout the western world. Tom Mosser was murdered by Ted Kaczynski known as the Unabomber, a psychopathic monster, angry at everyone. Mosser, Ted Kaczynski's last victim was killed in his home after opening a package delivered by the U.S. Postal Service as it exploded killing him instantly. After the funeral mass and burial Neil was approached by Burson-Marsteller's chief of European operations who resided in London. He thanked Neil complimenting him on the eulogy, and invited him to visit if he was ever in London, which as it happened was a month away.

One evening while in London Neil and I found our way to the executive's beautiful Mayfair apartment where he and his wife resided. After cocktails we were driven to a Persian style Indian restaurant, which was housed in an elegant townhouse with understated modern décor, and obviously expensive, since the menu didn't show any prices. Actually we didn't order from the menu. Delicate foods were brought on fine China plates for us to try, and having been advised in advance of my non-meat diet there were a preponderance of unusual plant-based foods with delicious sauces. It was an amazing evening, and we learned that the public relations company actually represented England's royal family, which kept them quite busy as more of the family members found themselves in trouble, in all sorts of ways to the delight of the British public.

All Saints Roman Catholic Church, located on 129th Street and Madison Avenue in Manhattan's Harlem section was in need of a pastor who could sincerely relate to the almost 100% African American members of the congregation. The Franciscan friary that had pledged to staff the church with Franciscan priests faced a dilemma because their declining membership didn't have anyone suitable and immediately available. Hence the call to Neil O'Connell, the priest with a varied background, a decade teaching in Historically Black Universities, and always relating successfully to everyone. Neil, transferred from St. Stephen of Hungary, after being there for nine years to All Saints the immense, Gothic Revival church that was dedicated in 1893 to serve primarily Irish immigrants residing in the immediate area.

All Saints Church was designed and constructed under the supervision of architect James Renwick, Jr., one of the most successful of all American architects. Renwick was raised in New York City, and was trained as an engineer at Columbia University. Early in his career in 1837 Renwick was an assistant engineer on the massive Croton Aqueduct project that brought drinking water from the Croton reservoir in Westchester County to New York City, a distance of 41 miles. However, Renwick was an artist and dreamer and was almost immediately successful as an architect. His most important projects were St. Patrick's Cathedral on Manhattan's 5th Avenue, the original Smithsonian Institution Castle in Washington, DC, Vassar College, Columbia University's Arts Library, and numerous hospitals and churches. All Saints Church was a Renwick masterpiece that was completed in 1893 containing a rich vaulted interior, and the last massive pipe organ manufactured by Frank Roosevelt the master church organ builder of the 19th Century.

Neil settled in as administrator and pastor, and invited us to All Saints for holiday celebrations mixed together with the Catholic mass, from time to time. The joy and obvious pleasure experienced by the parishioners of All Saints confirmed the positive history of the Black Church in America originated after the end of the Civil War at the start of Reconstruction. The Black Church, usually Baptist or African Methodist Episcopal, was the only part of the former slave's community and culture that could not be controlled by Black Codes and southern vigilantes. There were tragic circumstances of course, churches were burned down, and church attendees murdered. Dr. Henry Louis Gates, Jr. summed up the Black Church's vital role in maintaining the actual life-force of the African Americans. Dr. Gates wrote, "The Black Church was the cultural cauldron Black people created to combat a system designed to crush their spirit."(5)

After seven years, it was time for Neil to leave All Saints. He was having health issues, and needed a knee replacement. His congregation adored him and held a party in Neil's honor. Kathleen, Jonathan and I attended. The mass was enriched by traditional African American singing and joy. We all hugged several times, and everyone appeared happy and glad to be in the church. A joyful noisy congregation was enjoying the warmth and friendship offered by the communal experience, led by a white pastor, who brought out the goodness of people who originally had the right to be suspicious of his commitment to them. During the farewell luncheon for Neil, which had several hundred attendees and was slightly chaotic we sat with, and got to know Father Christopher Keenan a Franciscan friar. Father Chris had recently been appointed chaplain of the New York City Fire Department following chaplain

Father Mychal Judge's death at the World Trade Center on September 11, 2001. Remarkably Father Chris officiated at the funeral mass of my wonderful longtime friend GEORGE BUSIGO in Valhalla, NY almost a dozen years later. George and I met in Port au Prince Haiti while visiting the Caribbean around 1960. He was an electrical engineer, a dreamer of possibilities, superb athlete, great husband to Barbara, an outstanding dad, loving grandfather, and one of the best persons I have had the good fortune to know.

After his seven years at All Saints, Neil essentially retired from parish life. Due to the fully occupied Franciscan friary located on West 31st Street in Manhattan, upon leaving All Saints Neil moved into quarters of St. Joseph of the Holy Family Church, on West 125th Street in Harlem, but stayed in close touch with activities at the friary in midtown. The friary operates two hotels nearby for homeless people, and raises funds for their meals and clothing under the St. Francis Friends of the Poor project. For several years, Kathleen and I held large gatherings at our home prior to Christmas. Our guests were asked to bring packages of men's underwear and sox for the residents of the hotels, which are the most needed articles of clothing. We usually collected over fifty packs of new clothing, including designer underwear and sox from Saks 5th Avenue, always contributed by our generous friend DR. ALICE PIANFETTI.

St. Joseph's Church, Neil's new residence, was founded in 1860, and is the oldest church in Harlem. Now a Black Catholic parish it was originally founded for German Catholic immigrants. It's a simple red brick structure that recalls its rural origin when Harlem was a suburb covered with trees and greenery. St. Joseph's still maintains a small healthy green lawn in front on 125th Street, and several full shade trees that have somehow survived the bus and automobile exhaust for over a century. Neil lived for eight years on the ground floor of the rectory with an entrance from the garden, in a smaller space than he had at All Saints or St Stephen of Hungary.

Neil had hundreds of books. He read all the time when he wasn't teaching or ministering. He even read the books I wrote, much to Kathleen's chagrin. Also, he accumulated a large collection of photographs from the weddings he performed since his days at Fisk and Meharry. Among the photos were images of Kathleen's and my wedding performed by Neil in 1991 in Spring Lake, New Jersey. When I visited Neil for the first time at St. Joseph's I was upset by the small space he had been allocated. I was ready to complain to the pastor reminding him just who Neil O'Connell was, but Neil in typical Franciscan fashion calmed me down, and assured me he was comfortable, and liked the church's location near all sorts of public transportation, and what he always referred to as "reliable" restaurants. He loved public transportation, and took the subway system to the Bronx twice a week to Lehman College where he taught history now that he was retired from daily church life. He often visited with us in New Jersey, and at our lake house in Lake Ariel, Pennsylvania. My three children also got to know Neil quite well. He attended Betsy's wedding to David and gave an ecumenical blessing.

Neil and I sometimes spoke about Seton College, and Mary Ellen. We agreed she was brilliant (Fordham University Ph.D. in English Literature), but naïve, and trusting at times the wrong people. She loved the college, and the Boyce Thompson estate, but couldn't keep it from disappearing. There were ways to maintain some parts, and the Seton name, and the property, but once Mary Ellen's mind was made up there was nothing anyone could do to change it. Neil sometimes brought up the art auction story, which was priceless, humorous and ultimately quite sad. In order to maximize income for the college, we rented out the Manor and other spaces for weddings and other celebrations. The reception for my sister-in-law Maureen's marriage to Victor Marshall was held there. There were photo shoots, movies and commercials. Cellist YoYo Ma was actually filmed in a television commercial, in the Seton gym. Strangely Mary Ellen did not permit anything to be removed or hidden away for safekeeping during the events held in the Manor almost every weekend. In all of the time, over several years, the only missing item was an oil painting of a man's profile measuring about twelve by sixteen inches.

Due to the connection with Christie's auction house, the Seton art department regularly received copies of their current auction catalogs, and one morning, an agitated art professor launched herself into Mary Ellen's neat office with the current catalog. She pointed to a photo of a painting ready for auction, in about two weeks, and exclaimed that it was the missing painting. Mary Ellen immediately telephoned Walter the chairman of the board of trustees. The chairman was a partner in Mudge Rose Guthrie and Alexander, Mary Ellen's father's old law firm. She told him about the terrible situation, and he called Christie's. Not wanting to tangle with Mudge Rose Guthrie and Alexander, Christie's withdrew the painting from the auction. About five months later, the same art professor, now with a new Christie's catalog, showed Mary Ellen that the painting was for sale again. This time Christie's was armed with paperwork proving provenance from the painting's owner in California. The board chairman, could not dispute the ownership, and the painting was going on auction in two days. Mary Ellen was leaving for Florida to visit family the next day. She called me into to her office, and explained the situation. She instructed me to attend the auction at Christie's in Manhattan, and buy the painting by bidding no more than twelve thousand dollars. I was dumfounded. I had been doing everything and anything to bring revenue to campus, including selling IBM on the use of the entire dormitory, which needed a great amount of renovation for summer interns working at the IBM complex located near White Plains. My protests were ignored so two days later I showed up at Christie's on Park Avenue.

After about ten lots were bid on the painting of the man's profile came up for sale. It quickly was run up beyond my twelve thousand limit. I had the opportunity to bid only once, and was relieved when it was bought by someone else. The painting sold for fifteen thousand as I remember, with a buyer's premium of 10% added. That night Mary Ellen called from Florida. She sounded happy. "We have the painting back. I'm glad." I couldn't believe what I had heard. "No, Mary Ellen," I said. "I was outbid." Then the surprise. "It was bought by Walter. He was on the phone bidding, and his bid won." So, the board chairman and I were bidding against each other, but that wasn't the worst part of the story. A week later, after Christie's was paid, the painting was delivered to Mary Ellen's office. She was excited and called the art professor to see the painting that was back in the college's collection. The professor showed up and happily picked up the painting, and then put it down saying, "In our painting, the face is looking in the opposite direction."

Over the time of our friendship, Neil and I spent many times long into the night talking about politics, history, philosophy and anything else that caught our attention. But, never about our different beliefs. Neil is the true Christian concerned about everyone struggling to have a peaceful life, and fully accepting of other ideas, beliefs or in my case, no beliefs at all. He respected my Jewish atheism, and never saw a need to ever discuss it. He understood from the beginning of our friendship that my unbelief was as authentic as his belief. Here we are seemingly two people with opposite philosophies of life, but completely in sync with each other. Therefore, the day he called to say he was leaving the church in Harlem, where I often went to bring him to New Jersey, and was moving to the Franciscan friary retirement center in St. Petersburgh, Florida, was devastating to me.

Kathleen, Jonathan and I had a day together with Neil at our home, and later I drove Neil back to Harlem. The next day he was taking the Amtrak train to Tampa where he would be picked up by a driver from the Franciscan residence in St. Petersburg. I asked Neil how he will get to Pennsylvania Station on 33rd Street in the morning? When he said by subway with his luggage I lost it, and began yelling. "NO, no I said, no subway. I will drive you or you'll take a cab." He agreed, and promised he would taxi to the station. Neil always kept his promises. We stayed in touch by phone, and after two years, Kathleen and I visited Neil in Florida. He was happy to see us, but it was obvious that the Parkinson's had progressed. Therefore, we were relieved when Neil called a few weeks after our visit to give us his new address in Allegany, NY at the St. Elizabeth Mother House just a few streets away from his beloved St. Bonaventure University. After seeing Neil in St. Petersburg, we visited with LINDA AGRAN, a longtime friend from Ryebrook, NY in Westchester County now residing in Florida. To complete the circle, Linda reminded Kathleen and me that Neil had performed the marriage ceremony for her daughter Laura to her husband Keith Clancy about twenty-five years ago.

Four years later due to the Covid pandemic interrupting everything, Kathleen and I were finally permitted to visit with Neil in Allegany,

NY on March 21, 2022 at St. Elizabeth's Mother House. We were invited to see Neil by Sister Mary Lou Lafferty the administrator who had brilliantly kept the facility Covid free, and for the first time permitted visitors. The giant building is the cleanest place I have ever experienced. Neil's nurse Lynn brought us to Neil's floor, and then Neil in a wheelchair dressed neatly was brought to us in a pleasant parlor. Lynn is just wonderful, and caring, and everything you would hope for in an RN. Neil looked well, but wasn't responsive. I held his hand and we spoke to him for about thirty minutes. Lynn took Neil back to his room, and then showed us out of the building. The morning of March 25 just four days later Sister Mary Lou called to inform us that Neil peacefully passed away last night. Peaceful is the best way to describe my dearest friend, Father Neil.

The memorial service for Neil, celebrated at the St. Bonaventure University Chapel on April 2, 2022 was elegant, and modest embodying the Franciscan spirit. I could not process the fact that we were at Neil's funeral. We had not been directly in touch for some time. The letters I sent almost weekly with photos and clippings attached were read to Neil by his nurses. The disease had shut down his ability to speak or even read about two years before. Perhaps I was waiting for an emotion to crash down on me signaling that the best friend in my life was gone, but that didn't happen. Neil will always be in my thoughts as if I still can reach out to him.

Father Dominic Monti, OFM offered the Homily, a review of Neil's unique humanistic life. Father Dominic is a medieval scholar, and retired professor, and he spoke from the back of the Chapel's floor rather than from the high alter. The one hundred of us listening were swept into sharing parts of the life of the extraordinary Father Neil James O'Connell, OFM. Father Dominic said, "Neil made us better. He expanded our order's work to help those we hadn't known who need care and comfort." The service concluded with the Jewish Kaddish the prayer for the dead, as specified by Neil a year prior to his passing.

(5) *The Black Church: This is Our Story, This is Our Song.* By Henry Louis Gates, Jr., Penguin Press.

Chapter 6

Faces from a Good Life

Is it unusual, when one says, I have had a good life? I can't answer my own question since I know I have had a great amount of happiness and good luck for a big majority of my time so far on this earth. My family set the foundation, and I know how fortunate that has been for me. I also have happy pleasant memories from times with the good folks I have known through one of the passages taken in connection with my education, career or a lucky break for me getting to befriend people so outstanding that my life has been positively influenced by them. Following are several "Faces" from my life. They are the most humanistic people I know, and my life was improved greatly by knowing them. Thank you, my dear friends, for being kind, smart, and creative and especially for sharing your lives with me.

<hr />

Dr. Angela Cristini

I resigned from Seton College's administration in 1988, and secured the position, Director of Grants and Sponsored programs, at Ramapo College of New Jersey. The college, unlike the rest of the state's colleges with the exception of Stockton University, was newly formed.

The other state colleges and universities had been long time former teacher training institutions. similar to the state colleges in New York. However, unlike the SUNY system in New York that wove together all of the state's public colleges and universities, New Jersey's public colleges are essentially unrelated to each other. Rutgers is the actual state system of higher education, and is completely without ties to the other public colleges. Ramapo College had a lazy process of grant seeking that was occasionally faculty driven in science, but not much else.

One day early in my career at the college, while in my office in the academic complex a smiling petite woman wearing a white lab coat appeared. Her question concerned my knowledge of the then new FedEx service, which I actually knew about, and asked how I could help. The lab coated professor was DR. ANGELA CRISTINI a nationally known biologist specializing in marine science. Dr. Crisitini, needed to send specimens of crabs packed in dry ice to a lab in Minnesota. I helped her with that even packing the specimens securely, and summoning FedEx to pick them up. As the last line goes, in the film *Casablanca*, "That was the beginning of a beautiful friendship."

For the next quarter century, Angela and I worked together establishing a system of grant seeking from the federal government, New Jersey, and foundations and corporations. She became the example and inspiration to other members of the college's faculty not only in the sciences, but humanities, nursing and social science. I attended a private luncheon one time in Washington, DC at the Dupont Circle Hotel. The host TIM HANSON an important consultant to grant administrators, in higher education, had invited about a dozen of us to hear the latest initiative from the National Science Foundation (NSF), the largest funding source for research programs in science for American colleges and universities. The speaker carefully outlined the new program that would pay stipends to elementary and middle school teachers for their participation in learning more science, in order to improve their teaching, and inspire young people to consider science as a career.

The material in the proposed programs would be presented using new remote technology that had recently been developed and offered over the World Wide Web. One of the most important parts of the speaker's message, and we all promised to keep it confidential was that the NSF would not fund projects from colleges of education. They did not want to include teacher training institutions in the program since it was unfortunately obvious that teachers had generally been poorly prepared to teach science. Angela Cristini was exactly the kind of faculty member the NSF was seeking to lead the new initiative, a tenured full professor of biology, Ph.D. in biology and post doctorate in marine biology, successful teaching and advising of undergraduates, highly organized with an extensive research agenda and proven ability to write cogent grant applications.

Angela without any hesitation, began to develop our initial proposal to the NSF, which resulted in six million dollars in grant funding over the following five years from the NSF, and the federal Department of Education for the new program called teacher enhancement. Our college was paid an additional 52% of overhead for the program's operation. While directing these far reaching projects, Angela, created the first Master's program in educational technology that attracted school teachers and other professionals from throughout the region. The Master's program became the largest and most important graduate program Ramapo College had ever offered. When the Obama administration made available carefully managed grants, for the construction and renovation of science labs on college campuses, Angela, and I developed a proposal for $2 million to create a new biology lab, in the old poorly designed science building on our campus. We were successful, and the project was funded, and became the inspiration for a total renovation of the building, which was years overdue. Angela during her more than forty-year career at Ramapo College secured at least four times the external funding than the entire faculty together was awarded during the same period, over $44 million. Her continuing record of grants to the college will never be matched at any college by a single professor, with the exception of the giant research universities, where biomedical research on cancer and other life threatening diseases take place, or the physics projects for propelling spacecraft further into the solar system.

Not resting on her amazing accomplishments Angela and I attended our first meeting at the New Jersey Meadowlands Commission. The meeting was called by the Commission's Executive Director **ROBERT CEBERIO** who more than anyone was responsible for turning the vast Meadowlands marsh, from an infamous trash dump, into an ecological oasis in the center of New York and New Jersey's urban sprawl. The Commission had operated a public education program for several years, and at the time was seeking a new contractor to do a better job and attract more students, and other members of the public to the Meadowlands. Some faculty members of Ramapo College's Environmental Studies major also were at the meeting as well as they believed the program should be housed in their department, which would have proved to be a disaster and an embarrassment for the college.

While Bob Ceberio outlined his vision for the new program, Angela, assured me that it was completely possible to accomplish what was required. The faculty members felt the same way, but when asked to produce a proposal for the million-dollar annual project their answer was, "We may be able to get it together by September." It was March. Bob Ceberio, looked at us, and I said, "Two weeks." Angela, prepared a detailed proposal, and I developed the million-dollar budget, which was submitted at the promised time and accepted. Included about a year later in the Meadowlands Environment Center's program was specific outreach to students with disabilities. Angela enticed the college's director of specialized services JEAN BALUTANSKI to join the Environment Center's staff, and develop a new program for students with special needs. Presently that program would be mandatory, but twenty years ago, Angela, was a visionary.

BOB CEBERIO became a great friend and colleague of Angela, and me. He was the most respected public official in the entire Meadowlands Region, and after twenty-nine years with the Meadowlands Commission Bob retired because he knew his work was done there, and that he could move on to other projects that would provide great benefits to the residents of northern New Jersey. Throughout his career in public service, Bob taught graduate classes in public administration. He created the land use and management consulting firm RCM Ceberio, and immediately gained important clients who with Bob's help have increased the commercial and warehousing potential of New Jersey, and added hundreds of well paying jobs. Throughout my son Jonathan's undergraduate years, he worked remotely as a researcher for Bob's company. The experience was invaluable, and following Bob's example Jonathan completed a master's degree in public administration. After our being associated for several years Bob Ceberio, and I wrote the definitive book on the history of the Meadowlands.(6)

To date the Meadowlands Project has welcomed over 150,000 school students to the daily program, and several thousand adults to evening and weekend events. Ramapo College has received about $26 million in funding from the Meadowlands Commission. Angela Cristini never seems to tire. Her successes lead to more successes, and over her many years at the college Angela has created, and received external funding for another dozen science based educational projects located in school districts, and at the newly designated National Historic Site at Paterson's Great Falls. She has made presentations to President Clinton and the National Academy of Science, and is a reader of proposals for the National Science Foundation. Angela was the college's Vice President for Development two years, and has been brilliant in the position. She returned to the biology faculty in June 2023, and continued creating new innovative science education projects. The initial project is the enhancement of *Vertical Farming* a pioneering hydroponic solution to growing food, in a limited urban space tended by adults with special needs, who will develop careers in the indoor farming business.

(6) *New Jersey Meadowlands: A History by* Robert Ceberio & Ron Kase, The History Press

REED/Ramapo Vertical Farm & Certificate for Autistic Adults

Press Release

MAHWAH, N.J. – Ramapo College of New Jersey will receive $455,000 in funding to support a special environmental sustainability program that will create a vertical hydroponic farm and allow for the creation of jobs for young adults with autism as well as a valuable learning experience for Ramapo College students. The grant, included in the $1.5 trillion Fiscal Year 2022 government funding bill recently passed in the Senate, was announced by U.S. Senator Cory Booker (D-NJ) who worked to secure federal funding for critical New Jersey programs, projects, and priorities.

"We are so grateful for this funding which will provide valuable work experience for young people with autism as well as Ramapo students," said Dr. Angela Cristini, Professor of Biology. "The vertical farm will help prepare the workforce for this growing industry in New Jersey."

Ramapo College and the REED Foundation for Autism entered into a partnership that provides job training, volunteer opportunities, and paid employment for adults with autism so that they can live a more independent, fulfilling life. The College will work with REED to incorporate existing courses for the certificate program, which will be open to both higher-functioning young adults with autism and currently enrolled Ramapo College students. Funding will also be used pay up to 10 adults with autism to participate in paid job training in the farm.

Details for the funding include:

*Purchase and installation of repurposed shipping containers that have been converted into pods for vertical farming;

*First year's operating costs (seed, growing medium, fertilizer, utilities, and salary and fringe benefits for the farm manager);

*Incorporate existing Ramapo College courses to create a certificate in environmental sustainability, and to pay up to 10 participants with autism who will work in the farm.

"The projects funded in the government spending bill will provide major benefits to communities across our state," said Sen. Booker in a release. "I fought to ensure this funding was included and am grateful for the organizations, community leaders, and elected officials who joined together to advance these vital initiatives. As these projects all across New Jersey move toward becoming a reality, I look forward to seeing the positive impact they will have on local and regional economies and the improvements they will bring to the quality of life for New Jersey residents."

The farm will be made from recycled shipping containers that have been repurposed for vertical farming.

Dr. Ann T. Flynn

Early in my career while a faculty member at CUNY, I developed a collegial relationship with a Professor of Nursing who was completing a doctorate in psychology at NYU. ANN T. FLYNN was a brilliant and enterprising person with a sharp mind and subtle Irish wit. Ann also had a fine sense of fashion, and was always stylish. She was an attractive woman who looked many years younger than her age, which she admitted to me she lied about. At one point Ann left CUNY and became the assistant director of the Office for the Aging of Brooklyn's Catholic Charities. In that role, Ann saw firsthand the issues that surrounded aging in America at the time, especially in urban settings. On occasion, Ann would speak to my classes in sociology and social aspects of poverty. She returned to full time teaching after five years with the Office for the Aging when she accepted an associate professorship, in the graduate program in Gerontology at the New School for Social Research now known as New School University.

It was at the New School where Ann attended a lecture by Dr. Robert Butler a psychiatrist who had actually developed gerontology as a new field of study. Dr. Butler had written the first non-medical book on aging *Why Survive? Being Old in America,"* which was awarded the Pulitzer Prize in 1976. Ann became an acolyte of Butler, gathering data for his studies, and working for other psychiatrists, who had elderly patients they didn't know how to help. Butler was the first director of the National Institute of Aging, and is credited with coining the term "ageism." He left Washington, DC, and joined the Mt. Sinai Medical Center's School of Medicine in New York City creating the first Department of Geriatrics, at an American Medical School. In *Why Survive,* Butler painted a sad picture of aging in America. Social Security's monthly payments were modest in 1976, and recipients were barred from having a full-time job, while collecting the benefit. The additional benefit of the 401K plan didn't begin until 1978, and took a decade to become even somewhat popular. Therefore, in Butler's view, growing old in America for working class people, meant growing old and living in poverty.

Ann Flynn understood the data she was amassing, and somehow knew years prior to the digital age that those who controlled data would control public opinion and public policy. She envisioned individuals of all ages, even the elderly, if they had access to the technology that hardly existed at the time, they could have enriched lives. The average life span of Americans in 1976 was 72 years, as opposed to average life span in 2022, which is about 80, and we are hearing about more and more individuals, living beyond 100 years in decent health.

Robert Butler could not have predicted the value appreciation of the residential real estate market in the northeast and Midwest. Homes of retirees were sold for several times their original purchase price, and new homes were acquired by them in Florida and the Carolinas for low prices, and lower tax rates, so retired people could live comfortably in a pleasant environment. Butler presented the elderly as a hopeless generation, but he didn't anticipate as Ann Flynn had that seniors would become committed to walking, exercise regimes, gym memberships and yoga sessions, while wearing the latest fashions in exercise clothing and foot wear.

Jane Brody the pioneering *New York Times* personal health columnist interviewed Ann in the early 1980s, and wrote a long column about her ideas and predictions for the nation's elderly population. Ann accurately predicted that the new personal computers that were then first being marketed would connect older people to families and friends in other parts of the country, and that once mastered could lead to money making productive activities for seniors rather than the dreadful factory work predicted by Robert Butler as the answer to financial distress of the elderly.

Ann Flynn was one of the smartest people I have ever known. She was an intellectual who read everything that came close to her varied interests. At one point Ann became interested in the work of Elizabeth Kubler-Ross, the author of the 1969 book, *On Death and Dying.* Kubler-Ross, a psychiatrist developed a way of looking at death termed, "Five stages of grief," which has become known as, the Kubler-Ross Model. Ann incorporated Kubler-Ross' work into her teaching because she knew that American's were, of course, uncomfortable when dealing with death of loved ones. Perhaps, Kubler-Ross's, most important contribution, was her pioneering of the international Hospice Movement. Prior to her campaign for dignity at death, there wasn't a protocol for the dying even in hospitals or long term care facilities, and formal assistance for anyone dying at home was non-existent. Ann lectured on the establishment of hospices, and was responsible for helping to introduce the concept to the nursing profession.

Ann and I wrote a book together, *The Later Years* published by my friend MARVIN KARP who had acquired a spin off company from Harcourt Brace where he produced texts and audio-visual material, for high school and college courses. Our book had modest distribution, and certainly wasn't anywhere in the class of Butler's *Why Survive?* Ann retired from college teaching after a long career that inspired countless nursing students, and others who had taken her classes on gerontology. She had begun to write her views on aging as a book she titled *You Will Survive: A better plan for growing old.* At that point she had broken with Robert Butler's theories believing they were based on too small samples of aging people, and without considering the great societal changes currently under way. If she completed a manuscript I didn't read it, and I asked Ann's brother Jimmy the executor of her estate about the book. He said he hadn't heard of it, and as far as he could tell it wasn't saved on Ann's personal computer.

Marvin Karp

MARVIN KARP had the calm and rich voice of a radio announcer before the era of Howard Stern's whiney annoying voice became acceptable. Marvin was an alumnus of Columbia University, and had also earned a graduate degree from the Columbia School of Journalism. We lived nearby each other in North Tarrytown, NY. I don't remember how we met, and became good close friends. Marvin was at least fifteen years older than I was. He was married, and had a teen age son. Marvin was a writer and creator of audio-visual material for schools and college courses that were popular before the internet and technology rendered his products obsolete.

When his company was dissolved, Marvin moved his office from Pleasantville, NY, to his friend Mike Cicale's graphic art business, in an historic building in Ossining, NY. He did some freelance writing, and when I suggested he partner with me in producing short run periodicals for a few organizations with whom I had contacts, Marvin readily agreed. Of course, that was prior to the great shift to online magazines and annual reports, which decimated the graphic arts and printing industries. Since I was the full time Associate Vice President for Academic Affairs at the college, and still occasionally taught an evening class, Marvin ran the publishing business. Our most important and longest work was with New York Medical College, publishing its alumni magazine, *Chironian*.

New York Medical College has a glorious history of admitting women and minority group members to its classes for the study of medicine. The college began in 1860 in New York City, and in 1889 built The Flower Free Surgical Hospital, the nation's first teaching hospital owned by a medical school. New York Medical College was housed in the combined Flower-Fifth Avenue Hospital (where I was born) until 1971, when it moved to its present site in Valhalla, NY adjacent to the Westchester Medical Center, a comprehensive public hospital. After the move to Valhalla, the cash strapped Medical College, which had constructed a medical campus including modern housing for students, was acquired by the Catholic Archdiocese of New York in 1978. Facing great financial difficulties in the maintaining of churches and schools, over the following thirty years, the Archdiocese sought another sponsor for the Medical College and its system of affiliated hospitals, which were acquired in 2011 by the Truro College and University System.

Marvin and I, produced the *Chironian* for nine years thanks to our great friend JULIE KUBASKA, who had been the director of Continuing Education at Seton College before being recruited to the position of director of Alumni Affairs at New York Medical College. Julie was the perfect person for working with the medical college's alumni, who all were physicians at the time. Later on other graduate programs, in the health sciences, were established. She was always positive and smiling while being competent and efficient, which was necessary for dealing effectively with the varied egos of successful physicians. In time, the Medical College's Vice President for Development and Advancement left, and Julie was appointed to that position by unanimous consent of the alumni leadership, and the Medical School's administration. Her excellent relationships with the alumni, and other supporters aided her in bringing new ideas and new donors to the Medical College. Julie was also expert at planning and organizing highly successful events that brought in significant revenue for scholarships and research, which she continued to do for the rest of her fine career.

For a long time, the alumni magazine was written primarily by a woman from Manhattan who lived on the west side, wore hats, and was like a character out of movies made in the 1940s. After a while she retired, and Marvin and I wrote all of the material as well as arranging for the graphics, printing and distribution. The magazine's editor was a physician, a gastroenterologist practicing in a hospital in Westchester. Either Marvin or I would bring a pile of photos to the doctor's office in the hospital where he would carefully look over each one, and make his selections for the upcoming issue. Sometimes his office assistant would beg him to return to the clinical area where a patient, under sedation, was waiting for the doctor to begin a colonoscopy. I used to suggest to the doctor that he give up medicine and become a photo editor. I believe he was tempted.

Marvin and I had lunch together as often as possible even though I was at the college in New Jersey, and he was in Westchester, across the Tappan Zee Bridge. We'd meet at a diner in Tarrytown just off the New York Thruway. The diner is long gone, but when I drive by its old location, I always think about Marvin who was a wonderful friend. I looked forward to every time we met either for business or just to talk over lunch. He was a great conversationalist, and especially loved to tell stories about his little grandson, and son Andy, who followed his father and graduated from Columbia. Andy was a writer, in the fashion eyewear space, a specialty field, in which he was well known.

One day Mike Cicale, the graphic artist who helped produce our periodicals called to tell me that Marvin's wife Ruth had died, and that there would be a remembrance at a funeral home in Westchester, in two days at 10 am. Of course I attended but, for some reason, I didn't contact Marvin, assuming, of course, he would be at the service. Arriving at the funeral home, where the large parking lot had filled, I sought out Marvin. I couldn't find him, and when I saw his son Andy I asked where his dad was? Surprisingly, Andy said that Marvin was ill, probably with flu and stayed at home. I was shocked and concerned, and planned to call, and if he agreed, would visit with Marvin later that day. He always appeared to be healthy, and as far as I knew didn't suffer from any serious medical conditions, and saw his doctor annually for a physical, but rarely at any other time.

Someone called for quiet, and began a light funeral service, Marvin like me was culturally Jewish, but not at all religious. A eulogy was followed by many speakers, who had nice things to say about Ruth, which made Andy, his wife and young son smile. My thoughts were with Marvin, however, and wanted the session to end so I could call him. When all the speakers had finished, the funeral director who had been conferring with Andy, walked to the front of the long room, and said he had an announcement. Calmly he informed us that Marvin Karp, my fine, kind, dear friend had died at home during the remembrance for his wife. I've haven't quite gotten over not seeing Marvin that day. Especially since his immediate family decided not to have another memorial service for Marvin right after Ruth's.

Dr. Alice Pianfetti

Working in the beginning days of Open Enrollment at CUNY, was challenging to most of the members of the faculty. Students who had graduated from high school, but were unprepared in the basics of writing, math or even reading were flooding the city's public colleges. While the faculty applauded the expansion of college attendance, we also worried about students maintaining a responsible level of comprehension. At the same time, I was due for a sabbatical, and I took it for one year away from the college. Part of the time, was spent in Arizona, learning about the Navaho and Hopi Native Americans. I stayed at the Hopi Cultural Center in Second Mesa, Arizona, which was part visitor's center and part guest house. While there I received a telephone call from my father in New York. It was 1978, so cell phones were only dreams and fantasies of scientists and electrical engineers.

I learned that someone had called my parent's home looking for me, in order to offer a job at a university in New Jersey. In retrospect, I should have ignored the call, and not cut short my time with the Hopi. However, I was ready to leave, CUNY, after more than thirteen years there. The pay was low, and my commute from Westchester to Brooklyn, was becoming more difficult even though I didn't come in every day, which allowed me to teach, as an adjunct at other colleges. The new position was Assistant Provost at the Teaneck-Hackensack campus of Fairleigh Dickenson University, a private university, with about twelve thousand undergraduate students, on its three campuses. The person offering the job to me was someone I had known at CUNY, who had left there four or five years ago. I was flattered, to be remembered, which clouded my judgement. I accepted the job, and after a while learned that my new boss at Fairleigh Dickinson, the provost, was a criminal and a bully who after four years at the university was fired for grand larceny, and in today's environment, would have also been charged, with creating a hostile workplace and sexual harassment of female staff members.

However, during my time at the university, I was responsible for a myriad of departments, programs, and activities. I gained a great deal of experience, in the administration of a university campus, and worked closely with interesting and talented people. One of the first members of the administration I met was Dr. ALICE THOR PIANFETTI Dean of the liberal arts college. Alice, was one of the handful of true intellectuals, with whom during my career I had the good fortune to be closely associated. As an undergraduate, Alice attended Middlebury College founded in 1800, as Vermont's first college, then earned a Master's degree in French Language and Romance Linguistics from Fairleigh Dickinson University, and completed a Ph.D. in French Language and Literature at Fordham University. She's right up there with Leo

McLaughlin in intellect, and her knowledge of literature, especially the classics is unmatched by any of the faculty members, in any of the many colleges, in which I have taught. In addition, Alice, speaks and writes a half dozen foreign languages that include Swahili. Language and linguistics are the disciplines in which she taught during her fine long academic career. As a capstone experience, Alice, over several years, taught proposal writing in the Master's in Nursing Education program of Ramapo College.

Alice has been my close friend for decades. We went through our divorces, and family tragedies while in close touch with each other. Her brilliance is matched by her generosity, and caring for others, which introduced Alice to fascinating people, in other parts of the world. It was after her many times in Africa, where she connected emotionally with the people, the wildlife, and the land that inspired Alice to write *The Lost Wilderness: Tales of East Africa*. Alice, is a Fellow of the exclusive Explorers Club, and in 1998, participated in an Interdisciplinary Expedition on Easter Island co-sponsored by the Explorers Club. Alice frequently acted as interpreter for the group, since their marine specialist guide spoke no English as is the case with many Easter Islanders who spoke only Rapa Nui, the Polynesian *lingua franca* of the island or Spanish.

She has translated numerous scientific and technical papers for researchers. One notable translation project dealt with cave paintings, in Spain and southern France, depicting the prehistoric gatherings of honey. Another significant translation work was for *Huguenot Heritage*, a secular organization devoted to the history of French Huguenots, and their 16th and 17th Century French roots, and their subsequent contributions, to French and American culture. Alice Pianfetti's publicans include, *The Theatre of Nicolas Drouin dit Dorimon: A Contemporary of*

Moliere, and co-authored, *And the Champagne Still Flows,* a biography of Mme. Marie Rappold, leading soprano of the Metropolitan Opera from 1905–1920. Alice has had poetry and articles published in juried journals and magazines, as well as contributing to the *Comparative Linguistic Dictionary of Romance Etymology*. She is the past Chair of the New York Group of the Society of Women Geographers, and was Vice President, of their National Council. Always known to be involved in unusual and intellectual pursuits, Alice is a graduate of The Sommelier Society of America, and supports their ongoing study of oenology, and cuisine as related in different cultures. Recently while she was editing the manuscript of this book, I discovered, that Alice was a scuba diver and had done sky diving.

After writing about Alice Pianfetti, I had the good fortune recently to see her in person, now that Covid has been contained in New Jersey. I brought a copy of the book's manuscript for Alice to edit. We had lunch at The Farmhouse an interesting restaurant nearby to where Alice lives. She looks well, and has kept up her fine sense of awareness of political and societal happenings, actually better than most people I know who are half her age. Alice's' greatest source of pride is her granddaughter Kelsey's recent completion of a Master's degree in Public Health at Tulane University.

Carl Kraus

During my five years at Fairleigh Dickinson University as Assistant Provost, I was appointed Clinical Professor of Social Science, in the Dental School. The extra position meant delivering lectures to dental students on aspects of sociology, especially culture, race and class, as found in American society. Also, I officiated at some events for the students of the dental hygiene program, an excellent two-year preparation for preventive dental care practitioners. However, the most surprising aspect of my job was overseeing the campus radio station. WFDU, 89.1 FM was started in 1971, on the Teaneck campus of Fairleigh Dickinson University. At the time, I was informed that I was in charge of the radio station it was a mess in every aspect of its existence, and I wasn't even sure where it was located. The station's director was eased out, and a search for a FM radio expert was undertaken. The result of the search happily was the engaging of CARL KRAUS as director. Carl is steeped in the history and proper operation of FM radio. One day he brought me to the radio station's broadcast antenna the Armstrong Tower high above the Hudson River's Palisades in Alpine, NJ., which allows WFDU to broadcast over a sixty mile radius in New York and New Jersey. The 425 foot high radio tower was built by Major Edwin Armstrong in 1938. Major Armstrong who resided across the Hudson River in sight of the tower, in Yonkers, NY, was the creator of FM radio technology.

Carl changed the radio station's format, and attracted experienced volunteer radio professionals to host programs, offering many kinds of musical selections. He turned WFDU into a lab for students to learn practical broadcasting, the station's original mission. Carl, established fund raising events, and the listening audience increased, and supported the radio station. Over the years while working together, and during the many years since I left the university, Carl and I became good close friends. He is exceptionally smart, a kind and caring person who tells great entertaining stories, and he is a good listener, as am I, which I have discovered is the similarity that is found in all of my close relationships.

Ron Kase

In 2019, Carl, had an idea, a documentary film should be made about the Montclair Post Office murders that took place in 1995. We discussed the project several times, and we thought it would be a powerful message for gun control advocates, in our nation where assault weapon ownership increases every day. We wrote a film treatment with the working title *Sundown in Montclair* as a proposal to the documentary film makers, in New York City who Carl would try to engage in the project. Almost as soon as the marketing of our material began, Covid shut down almost everything in New York.

Carl is also one of the best proof readers I have ever known. He discovers errors missed by editors, and by me that would have proved embarrassing if they had gone uncorrected. His wife Ann, is an artist, a painter, and their son, Carl Jr. is a noted physician specializing in interventional radiology, a medical procedure that saves lives and enhances surgeries and treatments. Daily he had battled the Covid-19 pandemic, in the Emergency Department of the Columbia University Medical Center by treating patients unfortunate enough to require extraordinary care. Carl has a rich radio voice similar to Marvin Karp, which I only recently realized. They have other similarities as well, which is a compliment to both of them.

Carl Kraus is a keen observer of the media. Recently he mentioned that the January 6 Committee's visuals shown on television during the hearings were so well done they must have been managed by TV professionals. And sure enough, Carl sent me an article from the *Times* explaining that the former head of ABC News, and his team, sift through hours of depositions and vivid footage of the attack on the Capitol to put together the presentations seen by the public. The hearings prove without question that that Donald Trump planned the insurrection.

The treatment for the documentary, which Carl and I developed is shown here. Carl interviewed Montclair's retired police chief who was on duty the day of the tragic event in the branch Post Office, which made headlines throughout the nation, but sadly at the present time would only be another shooting in a public place. The unspeakable recent mass murders in a supermarket in Buffalo, NY, and the most terrible, and unbelievable tragic murder of elementary school children in Texas has not even been noticed by the Republicans in Congress, and certainly not by the leadership of the NRA, which only days later held their national convention in Texas. At the NRA cabal everyone including the victims was blamed by Senator Ted Cruz, but not the sale of human killing weapons and large magazines of bullets that kill more innocents quickly.

Sundown in Montclair (working title)
A Documentary Film Treatment
by Carl Kraus and Ron Kase
(In support of the desperate need for the control of firearms)
Introduction

Fairfield Street off of Watchung Plaza in Montclair, New Jersey hasn't changed much since 1995. It's a busy commercial place, parking is close to impossible, and on balmy days, the sidewalks are crowded especially when the schools let out for the day. However, late one day in 1995, March 21 to be exact the Plaza was the scene of chaos as police and medical personnel raced to 128 Watchung Avenue near the corner of Fairfield Avenue after reports of shots being fired in the small branch Post Office.

The Post Office door was tightly shut, and Montclair police officers broke it open using their shoulders. Once inside the narrow storefront, the police were confronted by a scene out of a slasher horror movie. The bodies of five men all hemorrhaging blood were on the floor behind the service counter. Miraculously, one of the victims, with obvious head wounds moved slightly and police and newly arrived medical personnel determined that he was clinging to life.

A New Jersey State Police Medical Evacuation helicopter was summoned. The craft touched down in the street near the Post Office, and the one victim of the assault who was still living was airlifted to Newark's University Hospital. Even though speech was impossible the victim was able to respond to questions asked by Essex County detectives and FBI agents by moving his fingers and toes. After extensive surgery he survived the ordeal and identified the killer of the other victims.

The individual carrying out the murders in the Watchung Plaza Post Office that day was 29 year old Christopher Green who had grown up in a middle-class family with a long and uneventful history of living in Montclair. Green had been a temporary employee at the Post Office for a period of nine months during the prior year, however, at the time of the murders he was employed by the Montclair Public Works Department. His motivation for the attack on his former co-workers and three strangers was, "crushing debt." Green actually returned to East Orange, NJ and paid off the rent he owed on his Executive House apartment with the stolen money, after committing the multiple homicides.

Faces from a Good Life

Scenes

Scene 1 Montclair, New Jersey, described by narrator, as upper middle class, artistic, highly educated, population, with over 37,000 residents which includes 30% African-Americans, making Montclair one of the state's most diverse towns. The setting for the novel "Cheaper by the Dozen" was set in Montclair its author's hometown.

Scene 2 Store fronts on Fairfield and Watchung Streets zooming in on the Post Office. Narrator describes the street's shopping culture which has traditionally resisted big box stores, and now hopefully can resist internet shopping.

Scene 3 The small post office is suddenly in focus. Inside the Post Office locals coming and going and a customer a long-time resident speaks about an event of 25 years ago. He still remembers the shock he felt that day, and asks, "Why are guns still so easy to get?" **(The statement sets the tone of the film)**

Scene 4 Enter Christopher Green, **(simulated).** Staff and customers lie down on floor after Green produces a pistol. Cash is scooped up and bagged. Green methodically shoots the 5 victims. One calls out Green's name. The postal workers were remembered as "sweet tempered men who never lost patience with harried customers." They were Ernest Spruill and Stanley (Scott) Walensky. The other murdered men, Robert Leslie and George Lomaga, were customers who had the ill fortune of being on the scene when Green began his slaughter. David

Grossman, twice shot in his head was the only survivor of the murder spree. **(Victim's photos are shown along with short bios by the narrator)**

Scene 5 Police Chief Thomas Russo on his way home after his shift responds to a radio message in his car that there were gun shots at the branch post office. The Chief drives immediately to Watchung Plaza and is the first one at the scene. **(Chief Russo on camera describes in detail what he found in the post office)** Montclair Police Headquarters. **(Simulated)** Emergency call answered and officers respond. Post Office door broken down. Carnage viewed. Ambulances summoned. **(Another statement from retired Police Chief Thomas Russo is emotional and descriptive.)**

Scene 5 One victim from the shooting David Grossman, still alive, is air lifted to Newark's University Hospital thus saving his life. **(Photos of firemen carrying the stretcher with Grossman to a waiting helicopter)** Narrator describes the scene in the Newark hospital as the medical staff scrambles to treat the one survivor of the Post Office shooting. **(Scene Simulated)** A current physician reviewing the chart and X-rays from the 25-year-old event speaks of the severe nature of the victim's wounds.

Scene 6 Officers from 5 neighboring towns and the FBI arrive on scene to begin manhunt for the shooter. Narrator describes the chaos in Montclair that day. **(Video footage from NBC, CBS or ABC is shown while Chief Russo on camera describes assembling the police resources.)**

Scene 7 In 4 days, Christopher Green, whose family has resided on Valley Road in Montclair for many years is identified as the murderer. Narrator provides some of Green's background, family history, siblings and parents, "A close loving family."

Scene 8 Chief Russo on camera describes in detail the apprehension of Green Green is arrested where he is living in East Orange in a high rise building. **(Simulated)** Statement by a psychiatrist who has studied Green and other unlikely murderers.

Scene 9 Interview and case review with Thomas J. Russo, retired Chief of Police of Montclair, NJ. Interview of Mayor Jackson, current mayor of Montclair. Comments by longtime residents have different views of the crime and the killer, and his guilty plea to avoid the death sentence.

Scene 10 Interview of present Chief of Police, Todd M. Conforti discussing how Green was able to legally purchase the 9 millimeter semi-automatic Taurus handgun he used to kill the victims. The Winchester Black Talon bullets Green specifically acquired for the murders were designed to do maximum damage to the human body. **(Thus, bringing up the issue of controlling guns that are designed and sold as lethal weapons only and are not sport rifles)**

Scene 11 Interview of Iryna Carey, daughter of murder victim George Lamoga and others who question how Green was able to legally purchase the gun and bullets and ask if New

Jersey law had changed. **(Discussion by a Brady Campaign to Prevent Gun Violence representative tying the event to the later escalation of gun violence even being carried out against school children)**

Scene 12 Interviews of current Montclair Post Office employees and local postmaster. Still shocked that Green was well prepared to do violence, and that he shot the victims in the head virtually guaranteeing their deaths.

Scene 13 Panorama of Montclair today attesting to the town's peaceful environment. Narrator reviews the crime and how Montclair survived its worst day. **(Brady Campaign official's statement supporting the control of firearms)** New Jersey's Governor Phil Murphy is shown in front of an out of business gun shop. His statement covers the history from the Montclair murders, and the then legal access to firearms and destructive ammunition to the present New Jersey gun laws, the nation's toughest

―――

Bob Lazell

When one reaches the age of four score, it has already become difficult or even impossible to establish new friendships. However, there are ways if one is a faithful user of Facebook, and is able to supply interesting and pithy material to one's Facebook page so that other interesting and pithy persons respond a relationship may be built. Or one may reside in a retirement community in Florida, and play golf, shuffleboard and bingo, regularly, and hang out at the community center's bar and restaurant. Friendships do spring up

Faces from a Good Life

in those places. I don't indulge often in Facebook except to see the posts of some good friends that mysteriously show up on my email. Also, and most importantly I don't reside in Florida the state with the second most stupid governor in the nation (Texas wins that one), and two bottom of the barrel U.S. Senators who actively work against their constituents. But I did acquire a great friend just a few years ago. BOB LAZELL, and I knew of each other's existence. We actually had met at some college events because Bob's wife is the equally amazing DR. ANGELA CRISTINI.

Bob and I had lunch together about five years ago to discuss some mutual interests. We now lunch every week at the Stateline Diner in Mahwah, NJ where we hold our "Policy Meeting" to settle the issues of the nation that need our attention. We are aligned in politics, humanism and intellectually except Bob is much more well read and is a computer wizard with the talent to make any kind of technology work. Bob was data manager for large medical studies carried out in hospitals in New York City and Rockland County, NY. He had to invent many of the data analysis procedures as the field was new, and innovation was necessary. Also, for a time Bob was Director of Digital Recourses for Tibet House in Manhattan. The organization is headed by Dr. Robert Thurman, Professor of Indo-Tibetan Buddhist Studies at Columbia University, and father of actress Uma Thurman. Tibet House projects record the history and culture of Tibet, in an attempt to preserve them, since the Chinese government is devoted to disassembling the small nation imbedded into China. Among his many accomplishments for Tibet House, Bob digitized three thousand photos of Tibetan life. He also was an antiquarian book dealer, for over thirty years. Presently Bob is vice president for technology for an international travel company.

Bob is a Jersey guy born in Englewood Cliffs, an upscale community not far from the George Washington Bridge, into a family of

Episcopalians. He participated in church youth group activities, and didn't question his family origins. He spent four years in the U.S. Coast Guard, and then graduated college as a biology major, while working as a laboratory technician, and remaining a member of the Anglican Church. I had read in the *Times* recently about an Episcopalian bishop who was found murdered, in his home on exclusive Shelter Island. Apparently the murder investigation revealed the bishop's murky past, and indicated that he wasn't the pure man of God as he had projected. I asked Bob if all Episcopal clergy were nuts because I had known a few? He answered, "Pretty much." Bob had strayed from all religion a long time ago. However, through *Ancestry,* the family history search service that provides an accurate record of one's relatives sometimes back many generations and centuries, he found out who he really is. In 1995 Bob was contacted by a cousin he hadn't known even existed. Her name is Loretto, and remarkably was a vice president of the new subscription service called *Ancestry*. She was contacting family members who had become lost from each other, but had turned up through her own search. Bob is a devoted internet researcher, and immediately became immersed in the quest to find out as much as he could about his own family's history.

BOB LAZELL'S roots, that had somehow become entangled with Protestantism, were easily traced back to Portugal, and the Sephardic branch of Judaism through his mother's side of the family. The Sephardic or Sephardi, which means Hispanic had resided on the Iberian Peninsula for centuries prior to the Alhambra Decree of 1492 announced by the Christian Monarchs of Spain, which expelled the Jews and Moors (Muslims) from Spain, and later from Portugal. Both groups Jewish and Moorish represented the highest level of culture, in the two countries. They were the architects, physicians, teachers and builders. The most famous form of Spanish and North African architecture is the distinctive Moorish style. After 1492, in Spain and a bit later in Portugal, members of both cultures facing either conversion or death left and settled in North Africa, and the Middle East. The Sephardic also found their way to Southern Europe especially Holland and France, and in smaller numbers to the Americas. The most iconic Sephardic names known best in the United States are: Montefiore, Sassoon, Monsanto, Cardozo, Maimonides and Bob Lazell's family name Seixas. The Seixas were Portuguese, and immigrated to Venezuela prior to settling in North America, after being condemned by the Decree of 1496 of King Manuel I. At the present time, an installation in Lisbon's main square memorializes the expulsion of Jews from Portugal at the end of the fifteenth century.

The Seixas family, became wealthy and influential in America, beginning in the 1700s through trade with Europe and the Atlantic countries involving banking and shipping. A Seixas family member participated in George Washington's inauguration, another in the establishment of the New York Stock Exchange, and the founding of Columbia and New York Universities. Bob Lazell's great grandmother Maud Seixas married outside of the Sephardic faith thus ending the ancient line that is traced back to Portugal. Remarkably Bob's father's family was also originally Jewish. His father's grandfather Moses Lazarus, an Ashkenazi Jew was born in 1875 in Troy, New York. The Ashkenazi are the Jewish people who inhabited central and eastern Europe in large numbers prior to the Holocaust. At some point in Moses Lazarus' life he cast off his Jewish origins, and became Joseph Arthur Lazell, a Christian. Therefore, between two and three generations ago, both sides of Bob's family rejected their Jewish beginnings. Bob and I speak about this often, and I admit to being envious because my family background is ordinary and boring by comparison.

Following up on his Sephardic background, which includes famous rabbis, diamond cutters from Amsterdam, and connections to other families with similar histories, Bob joined the Sephardic Genealogical Society with members in England, Wales, Amsterdam, and some in the United States. One of the Society's purposes is the transcribing of hand written diaries, lists, bills of lading, deeds, and other documents from the 1700s using a sophisticated computer program. The written material was salvaged from generations of the Sephardic who had left Spain and Portugal at the end of the 15th Century, and settled in Amsterdam, before moving on to other parts of Europe. The fragile papers have been archived in the Bevis Marks Synagogue in London, and the Portuguese Synagogue in Amsterdam. The Society was recently organized. Its mission is to become the repository of reference material for students, researchers, and scholars, who study and write about the complicated journey of a segment of the Sephardic people, after their expulsion from the Iberian Peninsula, a continuation of the Jewish Diaspora.

Bob and Angela reside in the charming hamlet of Valley Cottage, NY in a mid-18th Century home. Their house was a part of the property of a grand manor house built in 1751 now on the other side of the main road King's Highway, which runs through the former colonial residential tract. King's Highway has been a major north/south route for over 250 years, and is thought to follow the trail made by the Tappan tribe of the Lenape nation of Native Americans.

Bob is an excellent carpenter, plumber and electrician, which belies his Jewish roots. He has planed and supervised the installation of a completely new roof, a renovated kitchen and a swimming pool within their historic property. Recently we attempted to have a digital thermostat installed to control the central air conditioning in our home. After the installer gave up, we decided to abandon the project, but Bob took over, and accomplished the difficult installation.

The Lazell/Cristini's have for many years hosted a December holiday party attended by so many that one loses count of the attendees. Son Jeffrey, at all of the parties, is surrounded by a group of friends from his early years growing up in Valley Cottage who always participate in the annual event. Jeffrey is an international marketer, and distributor of professional level photographic equipment and software. He is an expert photographer, and a graduate of the Photography degree program of Drexel University. He's married to Jessica, and they reside in the exotic borough of Brooklyn.

Bob and Angela have become our travelling companions during the many pre-Covid trips to Mexico, Europe, and the Caribbean, and recently to Spain and Portugal, and last year to Ireland followed by Athens, the Greek Islands, and Sicily. The travel groups assembled by Kathleen also include the adventurous, DR. VICTORIA HOPE MADDEN a science curriculum expert, and the delightful and knowledgeable, HELEN BABITS a retired high school English teacher and Drug Education Coordinator, for the large Paterson, NJ school district. Vicki and Helen, are great and experienced travelers from whom we learn so much, and whose company is always fun and joyful. Bob was at first skeptical about travel that included sailing on cruise ships. Apparently his years in the Coast Guard serving on ships was quite enough sea duty for him. However, Bob has come around and has become a fine traveler and an enjoyable companion, while discovering the places we have been fortunate to experience.

Barry Zweiban

In the 1960s, it wasn't easy to stay in touch with friends or family, who lived in different places. AT&T was the only phone company allowed to provide service in the Northeast, and most of the rest of the country.

Telephone calls outside of a subscriber's zone were expensive. Long distance calls were very expensive. Letters and postcards written, and sent to friends, in even nearby locations were the most popular way to communicate. My moving away from Long Beach, NY where I had grown up, and gone to school had the effect of my never being in touch with any of the friends and acquaintances I had made and enjoyed for many years. My new circle of friends sprung from college relationships, and later from my career as a professor and college administrator. However, about eight years ago I responded to a high school graduates search platform that listed my high school, and my graduation year.

I put in my contact information, and to my happy surprise, I was contacted by classmate BARRY ZWEIBAN. Of course, I remembered Barry even though we were more like good acquaintances than close friends. What I remembered most about Barry was that he was always a pleasant really classy person, and a gentle soul despite the fact he was a member of our high school's varsity football team. In fact Barry, attended and graduated from college on a football scholarship.

Barry and his wife Jo-Ann who have been married for fifty-nine years left Massachusetts where Barry had retired from a successful career, and moved to Bluffton, South Carolina about seventeen years ago. It's interesting that both Jo-Ann and my wife Kathleen, are experienced travel agents. Barry, was involved with the food industry, primarily meat processing with vacuum packaging, and vacuum marinating. The company he owned was Cyborg Equipment, Inc. an international business, importing products from Israel, the Netherlands and Spain and equipment from Germany.

Barry and Jo-Ann, assured me they have adapted quite well to the different level of activity in Bluffton, South Carolina. They have a beautiful home located within of course a golf club community that boasts a good restaurant where we had lunch while visiting. Occasionally I email photos of winter weather to Barry reminding him that the white stuff covering everything is snow. He responds by telling me he's on his way to play golf, and that the temperature outside is 78 degrees.

Bluffton is located close to Hilton Head Island a golf and tennis mecca. Old Town Bluffton is listed on the National Register of Historic Places. The area's settled history dates back prior to the American Revolution, and later to the Civil War. When first settled by the British the entire area was a Proprietorship, in which the English Lord permitted settlement by the Yamasee People, a multi ethnic confederation of Native Americans. The Yamasee were an aggressive, slave trading clan who fought with other Native Americans, colonial settlers, and anyone else who happened to cross their path. Between 1715 and 1718 the Yamasee left, and settled in Florida's Indian Lands. The place that is present day Bluffton was designated "Devil's Elbow Barony" in 1718. The high bluffs of the May River probably were the reason that happily the settlement was later renamed "Bluffton." It was established as a commercial center in 1825, between two important ports, Charleston and Savannah. Bluffton is low country South Carolina, which had been a vast marshland, drained in order to grow rice and indigo in the 18th Century using the Gullah people who were slaves brought from Africa, for their expertise in farming. Decedents of the Gullah now reside in the low country, and today still speak their unique Creole English dialect.

I'm thankful to Barry, because he connected me again to our high school class members who all seen to live on Florida's East Coast. Jo-Ann is also a graduate of Long Beach High School, but many years later than Barry and me. Barry and Jo-Ann met in Long Beach when Barry missed the public bus that would have taken him to the Long Island Railroad Station, in the center of town. He was wearing a business style suit, white shirt and tie, and decided to try to hitch a ride. He put his thumb in the air, and a car stopped for him. It was Jo-Ann, whom he didn't know. They had a date that weekend, and were married six months later.

I have recently participated, due to Barry, in the fundraising for the Class of' '55 Scholarships awarded annually to two or three graduating seniors of Long Beach High School. The project is competently organized by our classmate Barbara Solomon. However, another significant connection I made through Barry was his informing me that our classmate JIMMY WAYNE has lived in Tarrytown, NY for decades, minutes from where I had resided for over twenty years.

With Barry and Jo-Ann, we toured historic Bluffton. The area is lovely, and reminds one that the Old South had beautiful places that survived even after generations of misery, and the most destructive war, in our nation's history. When Barry and I met up again, after over sixty years we immediately recognized each other, and happily Barry, is still the decent classy person I remember from high school. I'm indebted to Barry for re-introducing me to Long Beach, the place where I enjoyed growing up. We regularly exchange emails, and keep each other informed regarding the precarious state of our nation's politics. Barry has a great sense of humor, and often forwards pithy comments that I enjoy for several days. I look forward to visiting Barry and Jo-Ann now that travelling has resumed, and we can safely join friends everywhere.

James D. Wayne

At every stage show, sports rally and concert, throughout my years during Junior and Senior high school in Long Beach, NY we were treated to the distinctive melodies of the fabulously talented JIMMY WAYNE, and his trumpet. We all realized that Jimmy and music belonged together. I connected with Jim, whom I think of as Maestro James D. Wayne, after learning about his storied career in music. He is still the fine musician we knew in school, and became a teacher, arranger, director, and conductor of four significant symphonic orchestras, as well as a music entrepreneur. And oddly enough Jimmy and his wife Joan, have resided in Tarrytown, NY for decades, while I resided in what was then North Tarrytown, and now called Sleepy Hollow, NY. We lived less than ten minutes from each other, but I left there long ago. Until BARRY ZWEIBAN mentioned that Jimmy dwelled in Tarrytown, I would not have known he had lived nearby, and presently, we are only about twenty miles apart.

Jimmy was another good acquaintance from high school. His dad was one of the two doctors in practice in Long Beach at that time. I contacted him three years ago, and we have been in touch regularly ever since mostly by email, and telephone due to Covid. Jimmy has generously provided to us many of his CDs of Christmas music, and other themes. Joan and Jim live in a part of Tarrytown that is really in the town of Irving-on-Hudson, or maybe it's the other way around. Their home is an interesting mid-century modern house, built onto the side of a hill and overlooking a small lake that attracts ice skaters during the winter. Of course a music room added some years ago is one of the home's main features. Jim was a member of the Coast Guard, and has a love of watercraft. He keeps a boat on the Hudson River at a boat club on the Tarrytown waterfront.

In order to correctly characterize Jimmy as "The Music Man," I did some research on the internet regarding his extraordinary career in music. In the *Journal News,* of May 7, 2015, reporter Morey Storck wrote, "On May 9, Tarrytown and Sleepy Hollow will have the opportunity to hear and appreciate one of the nation's foremost wind and percussion ensembles.

This unique organization is called The Hudson Valley Symphonic Wind Ensemble. James D. Wayne is it's Music Director and Conductor. The Ensemble's membership is comprised of approximately forty-five unpaid instrumentalists from New York, Connecticut and New Jersey."

Through *Wikipedia,* I learned more about Jimmy's professional history in music. It lists his conducting positions including band director at New Rochelle High School, in the 1970s where his music program gained a national reputation to the level of playing a live concert on radio station WQXR the iconic classical music station in New York. From 1978 through 1981, Jim was Music Director and Conductor of the American Symphonic Wind Ensemble, and at the same time he was also Music Director and Conductor of the University of Bridgeport Symphonic Ensemble. An article in *The New York Times* on February 27, 2005 highlighted the fine quality of Jim's work. It said, "Mr. Wayne had set a high standard, creating musical performance of a more refined nature than most people would associate with a band."

In 1988 Jim co-founded, the Hudson Valley Wind Symphony a concert band performing classical music and traditional repertoire. He was the group's conductor and musical director until 2004. In 2005, Jim founded a new musical organization, the Hudson Valley Symphonic Wind Ensemble, which I'm happy to report is alive and well, and beginning to offer new concerts in the hopefully post Covid period we have now carefully entered. James D. Wayne is also a music entrepreneur according to writer Maury Storck, in the *Journal News.* In 1984, he founded *Second Hearing Records* one of the first commercial all compact disc labels. Since 1989 Jim has owned and operated *Silverdisc Productions* in White Plains, NY. The company specializes in the production and manufacturing of compact disc audio supplements for college music textbooks, which Jim has explained to me several times, and I still don't understand, the highly technical nature of the product.

On May 22, 2022 at Jim's invitation, I watched and listened, to the concert presented by the Hudson Valley Symphonic Wind Ensemble to benefit the Maryknoll Sisters of Ossining, NY. The Wind Ensemble is an orchestra of over forty excellent musicians led by conductor James D. Wayne. The musical presentation was elegant and perfect. As Jim strode to center stage to begin the program members of my generation would be reminded of Leonard Bernstein opening a concert at Lincoln Center. Jim modestly refuses to acknowledge any similarity between himself, and Maestro Bernstein, but it was evident to me. Standing straight, in his black tuxedo, with silver-white hair, and using solid gestures for cuing the musicians, Jim brought out the finest performance of many of the best concert musicians in our region. It was a stirring experience for the audience that was treated to exceptional music offered live, on a Sunday afternoon. I was thrilled to actually witness again music by Jimmy Wayne that is still remembered from a long time ago while in Long Beach High School.

Dr. Rich Lucanie and Dr. Anabel Lucanie

Partners in life, and partners in medicine defines RICH and ANABEL LUCANIE the leaders of one of the most important primary and family medical practice in Northern New Jersey. Doctors Rich and Anabel began practicing medicine almost immediately after completing their residencies in internal medicine at the affiliated hospital of New Jersey's University of Medicine & Dentistry. They married and moved to Ramsey, NJ, which was familiar to Rich, who was raised in Wood Ridge in the same county. Anabel was born in Spain, and grew up on the island of Puerto Rico where she excelled in high school, and graduated from the University of San Juan, and the university's School of

Medicine. After a fellowship at the National Institutes of Health (NIH) in Washington, DC, Anabel, began her internal medicine residency at the University of Medicine and Dentistry of New Jersey (UMDNJ) where Rich also was a resident in medicine.

Rich Lucanie always strived for perfection in everything he undertook. He played baseball and soccer, and applied himself to school work with the same drive to be the best at whatever he was doing. After high school, Rich entered The Rutgers School of Pharmacy, and graduated with a degree in the discipline as did two of his brothers. His superior academic performance led him to apply to medical schools, and after being accepted by several he began medical studies at the Downstate School of Medicine of the State University of New York (SUNY). Rich wanted experience in an urban medical setting, which he found daily in the gigantic Kings County Medical Center, where his clinical training began, and where he honed his skills as a diagnostician, which made another physician to whom I was referred say, "Rich Lucanie is a doctor's doctor."

Anabel and Rich, and three additional physicians, make up the medical team of the Valley Diagnostic Medical Center located in the Ramsey Medical Center on Franklin Turnpike. Their state of the art medical center has extremely loyal patients who are grateful for the excellent care provided, in an unhurried personal manner. So loyal are the Lucanie's patients that almost every time we have had dinner with Rich and Anabel, in a restaurant within ten miles of Ramsey, a patient would come up to our table expressing appreciation for their medical treatment by either of them.

Anabel's brother is a Brigadier General, in the U.S. Army Reserve, and has coordinated Puerto Rico's disaster recovery after the several tropical storms that have decimated the island during the last five years. The General's son and daughter have followed Aunt Anabel and Uncle

Rich, into the medical profession, and have completed residency programs, in New York for medicine and surgery. Rich and Anabel's adult children are as expected highly educated. Daughter Elena, is a psychotherapist practicing in Hoboken, NJ and son Richard recently completed a graduate degree at Georgetown University, and is employed by an international biotech company in Washington, DC.

Anabel and Rich, are wonderful friends, and are our caring doctors, for as long as we have known them. Our son Jonathan, and their son Richard played together while in elementary school, and later through high school on the soccer field. One of my favorite stories about them is a time during both of our son's Middle School years, and Rich an avid soccer player to this day was helping coach the boy's team. It was after the school day, and we were at a local field watching our sons play soccer. A woman, from nearby Saddle River whose son attended the Ramsey schools, said to Anabel who was standing on the sideline, "My husband can't come to the games. He's a doctor." Anabel, who was always polite didn't say anything, so I had to. I said, "See that coach across the field? He's a doctor. And meet, Anabel Lucanie, also a doctor." We didn't see that woman again.

I could go on and on, regarding the great friendship we enjoy, and excellent medical treatment we have received from Anabel and Rich, and I do whenever I speak about them. Last fall Rich, detected that I had a problem with my kidneys, which was subtle and had gone unnoticed by a specialist in that field. Rich immediately with some resistance from me, found treatment for me from a urologist soccer buddy late on a Friday afternoon that three months later led to successful surgery and elimination of the problem. Anabel saved the life of one of Kathleen's brothers who was staying with us while recuperating from a complex surgical procedure, but was additionally in need of heart surgery. After a phone call to her for advice, Anabel, showed up suddenly examined the patient and called for an ambulance for transport to Valley Hospital, which saved the life of Kathleen's sibling. Jonathan, always travels from his place, in Jersey City, to Rich Lucanie, when he needs a checkup or has a health issue. Earlier this year, the Lunacies became grandparents, and have a wonderful grandson, Leo. My gratitude to Rich and Anabel for their friendship, and wonderful medical care has no limits.

Deborah Solomon

Cuba had begun to emerge in 2014, as a place where if carefully planned, Americans could legally visit for the first time since the United States embargo of Cuba begun in 1962. Bestkase Travel went full steam ahead to bring travelers to Cuba, and after our first visit there engaged ILLIANA MARTINEZ a skilled Cuban woman who had the needed contacts and stamina to make arrangements, for our busloads of American visitors. Illiana worked with us until Trump, bowing to pressure from the Miami Cubans, shut down American visits to Cuba once again. Kathleen's company had acquired a license from the federal Department of Commerce to organize trips to Cuba for Americans with an interest in environmental issues. In 2015, Bestkase Travel brought sixty-seven visitors to Cuba, on a single trip. Among the varied participants was an individual to whom I had spoken on the telephone over several years as she represented the company that manages my 401K investment program, but we hadn't actually met in person. My telephone friend was DEBORAH SOLOMON.

Meeting Debby Solomon at Newark Airport along with about thirty members of our group assembled to fly that day to Jamaica was a little bit of a surprise. Debby wasn't whom I had assumed she was, a woman from the large Jewish Solomon family. Instead Debby is an African American Baptist with a Jewish sounding name. We flew to Ocho Rios, Jamaica to board a ship the following day to set sail to the island's second largest city Santiago de Cuba. At the time it was still not possible to legally sail directly from the United States to Cuba. Also Americans could not be classified as tourists. We were technically environmentalists on an educational mission. In Jamaica. We teamed up with the rest of sixty seven members of the Bestkase Travel group, including a college choral group, and its flakey conductor. Then our Greek owned ship sailed for a week's travel in and around Cuba. Debby is a very social individual, whose people skills were honed working in the investment field. She immediately connected with, DR. VICKI MADDEN, TERESE HENDRICKSON and ANGEL RIOS, our friends and fellow travelers. The Cuban experience was remarkable, and before returning to New Jersey, Debby asked Vicki Madden, who is a highly experienced educational projects director for advice on raising funds for her church's renovation, in Rutherford, NJ.

Vicki and I had worked together for many years on funded projects, so she suggested that Debby talk with me. I learned that Debby's interest was raising funds for necessary structural work on the church she attended in Rutherford. The Mount Ararat Baptist Church is an historic African American community founded in 1903, and then because they outgrew the original building the parishioners constructed the present church in 1916. I visited, Mount Ararat Baptist Church with Debby Solomon, and was completely impressed by the elegance and beauty of its chapel. It's an historic treasure with a fine polished wood interior, and the only century old building in Bergen County, NJ that was constructed as a place for African Americans. Even though the chapel space was in perfect condition there was an underlying structural issue, that impacted the integrity of the entire building.

Simply put, the church was built over a hundred years ago, on cinders and original earth. The building did not have a foundation of any sort, and that had to be rectified. Debby decided to take on the project of raising enough money, to fulfill the engineering requirements for installing a four inch thick concrete slab, with a vapor barrier, resting on an additional four inches of gravel. Together we prepared a needs statement, and proposals to several, New Jersey family foundations, and we attracted contributions, from individuals and local companies. Along with Debby, I attended several church board meetings to provide input on a variety of financial issues connected to the fund raising. At the meeting's end, we would all join hands, and the Reverend would lead us in a hymn. I enjoyed the feeling of community, a rare emotion for me, and mentioned more than once, if I wasn't an atheist, I'd join up with them.

Debby and I, prepared the application to Bergen County for historic status for Mount Ararat Baptist Church, which was granted. We worked harder on the application to the State of New Jersey also for historic status. However the Chris Christie administration, didn't believe that the last white shingled African American church, in the state, over a century old, the scene of presentations by well-known civil rights activists, and the repository of the history of African American's journey, from the South to New Jersey was entitled to historic status.(7)

I wanted to know, who is DEBORAH SOLOMON? I found that Debby's family came from Florida three generations ago, and settled on the North Fork of Long Island, in the Greenport area where they still reside. Debby attended public schools in Suffolk County until she left for college at Marshall University where she played Division I women's basketball. After graduating from college with a degree in Marketing & Management, Debby began a career in New York City in the insurance business, then joined a financial services firm and eventually the wealth management group of TIAA the largest investment company in the nation. "Teachers" as it's known by its employees, was started in 1916 by Andrew Carnegie as a fully funded pension program for college professors. The company is a not for profit corporation that manages over a trillion dollars of its member's funds. Their programs have expended over the years to include members in research, cultural, and medical and government positions, along with the original academics. Debby carved out a twenty five year career with TIAA while serving on the Rutherford Civil Rights Commission. She is well known and respected in Rutherford where she has lived for decades. Her son resides in California, and she has a grandson in Texas.

Debby, agreed to be an early reader of my novel *A Time in Ybor City* along with two other persons whose opinions I value. She actually wrote the part of the chapter that takes place in a hair salon in Harlem, one of the best scenes in the book that I consider my best work, which is under consideration for a feature film. Debby is well read, an intellectual, enjoyable for discussion of ideas. For a while I had hoped to work with Debby on a book for *The History Press,* which outlined the origins of African Americans travelling from the South to northern New Jersey during the "Great Migration," after the, Civil War. A parishioner of Mount Ararat Baptist Church has a vast collection of photographs, ephemera, and news articles. He has letters from Tuskegee Airman, Calvin Spann, and Daniel Rich both, Mount Ararat parishioners. Other churches that served, African American communities in our region also hold collections of materials that should be memorialized so that they are shared by researchers and the general public. However, due to different pressures the project didn't get off the ground much to the disappointment of the publisher and me.

My beliefs while being with Debby during the many project meetings with the church's leadership were confirmed. I of course, believe we are all alike. Everyone has highs and lows, sadness and happiness, frustrations and triumphs, and it doesn't or shouldn't matter what you are on the outside, because we are all the same, in many other ways. However that said, when will all Americans accept everyone who is trying to have a pleasant enjoyable life, achieving success, following community norms, and not tampering with the democratic process? Those of us on the Left thought we had made an important turnabout, with the election of the great BARACK OBAMA. However we watched in horror as the next president, a degenerate racist fool, quickly undid civil rights, voting rights, environmental regulations, housing programs, and anything else he and his party could do to minimize the power of African Americans.

As much as President Biden has restored what was eliminated in the vulgar Trump era, we have witnessed the obscene, obviously racist, treatment of the most qualified nominee to the U.S. Supreme Court, in modern times. I am mortified by the blatant, white supremacist, behavior of Republican Senators. I appreciate the opportunity Debby Solomon offered me, the chance to become closely involved with fine, intelligent people, whom I would not have ever known.

(7) **The History of the Mount Ararat Baptist Church** The borough of Rutherford, NJ was delineated in 1881, after being a section of various other municipalities. It is located on the edge of the New Jersey Meadowlands a vast eco system that has an agricultural history dating back to the Dutch settlers of Manhattan in the late 1600s. Rutherford developed as a bucolic village of private homes on

broad treed streets, small businesses and large monumental churches. Living in the midst of Rutherford's residential neighborhoods was a community of industrious African-American families that had immigrated from the South seeking a better life in New Jersey. **In 1903 the Black community sought to establish a Baptist Church in Rutherford. The village's elders refused to permit such a structure on Park Avenue, and offered a site for a church in the Grove Street neighborhood.** A church was built by the Black families living in the district bordered by Grove and Wood, Erie and Union Streets on a plot of flat land. After more than a decade of use, the building required extensive renovation, and had to be expanded to meet the needs of the growing congregation.

In 1916 a new Mount Ararat Baptist Church was erected at 27 Elm Street. The church has welcomed parishioners for over one hundred years without interruption. The Sanctuary has been carefully preserved, and the original pressed tin metal Victorian style ceiling is firmly in place. There are seventeen stained and leaded glass windows each designed by a distinguished artist that provide a cheerful and open ambiance to those visiting for the first time as well as for the members of the Mount Ararat Baptist Church assembly. The Sanctuary has provided a forum for visiting civil rights, political and cultural leaders, and continues to welcome speakers who have messages for the community.

The early congregants owned businesses and engaged in various occupations in Rutherford, providing services to both the Black and white communities. A livery stable was active for decades as well as blacksmiths, tailors, milliners, a catering service that prospered, and some worked as domestics in the large homes of Rutherford and for Iviswold Castle during the years it housed the Rutherford Union Club (Now Felician University) teachers and a pharmacist were among their ranks. **Tuskegee Airmen Calvin Spann and Daniel Rich were Mount Ararat parishioners**. For generations the church has been linked to other Black community organizations that sought to normalize the life experience of their members. Most notable were the Colored Voters Association founded in the 1920s, the Murray-Hodge American Legion Post 453, and the Colored Elks Club. Mount Ararat Baptist Church has been the unifying force for African-Americans in Rutherford for over a century.

Dr. Michael Riff

A surprising fact about DR. MICHAEL RIFF the historian, scholar and recognized expert on the Holocaust is that he loves cooking. He cooks almost every day. Michael, doesn't make simple dishes as I do when I have to cook something. He prepares dishes with ingredients that originated in Persia, India, China, Eastern Europe or Turkey. When he dines out it will almost always be in a restaurant representing one of the places, where he finds his recipes for cooking at home. During the last several years with interruption of course during Covid, Michael and I have had lunches at dozens of restaurants, for which he has searched on the internet, and by asking people who also are foodies for suggestions. The results of his constant hunt for great meals have usually been good, sometimes disappointing, but always interesting.

Michael Riff, was born in London, England, and grew up in Manhattan and Forest Hills. NY. His parents left their home in Czechoslovakia in 1939, just prior to the beginning of World War II in Europe. Refugee organizations aided them on their journey through Poland to the seaport from where they boarded the ship *Warsaw*, and sailed to England. After being relocated from place to place by a Czechoslovakian relief organization, they moved to the Notting Hill section of London as the war began. They survived the Blitz, the German bombing of civilian targets, in several British cities. In London, about thirty thousand civilians were killed by bombs dropped by German airplanes, and Germany's new weapon the V-2 rocket. Happily the Riff family remained safe, and with eighteen month old Michael emigrated to the United States in 1946, about a year after the war ended.

Michael and his parents settled in Manhattan. While living there they started a leather goods business that became successful by establishing a design, manufacturing, and retail operation, on the fashionable east side of the city. Michael's sister Carroll was born, and the Riffs relocated to Forest Hills. Michael graduated from Forest Hills High School, and entered Queens College of the City University of New York. He majored in history, drawn to it because of his European background. While at Queens College, Michael, met other campus students, Paul Simon, and Carole King. This became the pattern for the rest of Michael's life. He has met and become acquainted with, and developed friendships with many noted and famous people.

Upon graduation from Queens College, Michael was accepted to the University of London's School of Eastern and Slavonic Studies, as a candidate for the Ph.D. in History. This fit comfortably into his own history, and his ability to speak several languages. He selected The University of London primarily because his parents still maintained personal contacts with individuals in London from the time they lived there. The University was founded in 1836, and is the third oldest university in England, after Oxford and Cambridge. Also it's the first in Great Britain, to accept students regardless of gender, race, or religion, a revolutionary concept at the time.

Upon the earning the doctorate in history, Michael, began teaching classes at the, London School of Economics and Political Science, known worldwide as the LSE. He moved on to teach at the University of Essex, Colchester campus, an innovative place located about an hour from London near the historic town of Colchester, England's oldest recorded town. The University calls itself, "The most internationally diverse university on the planet," because it's the home to over 15,000 students, from one hundred and thirty countries. Michael, maintained contacts with people whom he had met during his doctoral work in London. Some were in the shadows of the British government. One day he received a telephone call from a former member of the SAS, England's version of the, Navy Seals or Army Rangers.

The caller was M.R.D. Foote, and he had the following message, "You will get a call from someone with a triangular life functioning among Washington, DC, New York and Paris." Foote while working for British intelligence units was known to have parachuted behind the German lines during the Normandy Invasion, known as D Day in 1944. Soon after Foote's call Michael was contacted by William Casey. Casey was of course the director of the CIA from 1981 to 1987. They met in London and after, a brief interview Michael was engaged as Casey's researcher for the book he was writing, *How and Where the War was Fought,* a history of World War II. Casey's book was published by William Morrow & Company, and is still a definitive resource for anyone interested in the accurate history of the war.

Casey was brought into the scandal that became known as the, *Iran-Contra Affair,* which led to indictments of some high ranking members of Ronald Reagan's administration. Michael, was concerned that Casey, the old warrior, would not be spared from the political blood-letting over Iran-Contra. Casey kept in touch with him, and tried hard to recruit Michael for the CIA. Whenever Casey was in London, Michael would meet him for lunch or dinner usually at Claridge's. Michael would drive Casey to meetings away from London that he regularly had with shadowy characters who could have been creations of John Le Carre. Michael's concern that Casey, was headed for, or was already in difficulty, proved to be accurate. Casey was felled, not by a political issue, but by a brain tumor. He died on May 6, 1987.

After teaching at three British universities, over several years, Michael, returned to New York and joined the Leo Beack Institute, now a part of the Center for Jewish History that's devoted to the history and culture of German-speaking Jewry. The affiliation, led Michael to the, Anti-Defamation League (ADL), one of the watch dogs along with the, Southern Poverty Law Center, and the American Civil Liberties Union (ACLU) that record and take legal action against politicians and organizations, trying to subvert the democratic process in America. He rose to the position of Associate Director of the ADL's New York office. Missing the academic life, Michael, resigned from the ADL, and accepted a faculty position at the University of Southern Maine in Portland.

Enjoying life in Maine, most of the time, Michael after three years, left the university to accept the directorship of the Center for Holocaust and Genocide Studies at Ramapo College of New Jersey, one of the oldest Centers of its kind on a college campus. Michael remained at Ramapo College, for twenty-five years, teaching and directing the Center's programs that brought internationally recognized scholars, authors, and journalists to the college, for presentations to the campus community, and the general public. He is General Editor of the *Dictionary of Modern Political Ideologies,* (Manchester University Press), and author of *The Face of Survival: Jewish Life in Eastern Europe Past and Present,* (Vallentine Mitchell & Co. Ltd.,).

I always enjoy speaking with Michael about Europe. He is completely knowledgeable about the continent's long history, its politics, culture, and ethic issues. My own background is in American history tied to my studies in sociology, which covers only about two hundred years. My father, whose parents originated from Eastern Europe, always avoided discussing anything about Europe during its dark period between the world wars. He wanted nothing to do with Europe, but had great respect for England because of its people's endurance during the Blitz. Until visiting some parts of Europe, I too had little interest in the countries that centuries ago sent out ships, armies and missionaries to divide up the rest of the world.

Michael, is married to, Jane, a data manager for KPMG, who also teaches data management at Ramapo College. Michael's son David, from his first marriage, resides in Berlin, Germany with his family. David is a writer, and senior curator, for the International Arts & Culture Festival, held annually in Graz, Austria.

Morton R. Covitz, Esq

On my first day as a sixteen year old freshman at Boston University, I sat in the front row of the auditorium called Hayden Hall where new student orientation was taking place. Sitting next to me was another freshman, also wearing a red and white beanie cap. I introduced myself to Morton Covitz, a tall confident appearing guy, who informed me he was a commuter student from Chelsea, Massachusetts. Morton and I joined the same fraternity, and became friends for the rest of our lives.

Mort became a highly successful attorney, specializing in real estate transactions, and commercial ventures. He always helped with my occasional issues that required legal representation. Mort had for twenty nine years been the Director of the New Jersey Supreme Court's Attorney Ethics Committee for Bergen County. It was a volunteer position coordinating the committee that provided the public with an important impartial venue, for the investigation of possible malpractice by attorneys. I served as one of two public representatives on the committee for a three year term, and was always impressed by the diligence of the members who were lawyers.

Mort retired, ending a stellar legal career that began with teaching at Rutgers Law School soon after receiving his law degree from Boston College. One Saturday, while I was visiting the Boston College campus with Mort, he introduced me to Farther Robert J. Drinan. Robert Drinan, who was the law school's dean, was a member of the Jesuit order. Morton as an editor of the *Boston College Law Review,* was well known to Dean Drinan. We sat in Father Drinan's office, and talked about the issues of the day. He was inspiring, and upon leaving Boston College at a later time, Father Drinan was elected to Congress as a representative from Massachusetts, where he served from 1971 to 1981. Congressman Drinan was an advocate for worldwide peace and justice and human rights, and was a fierce objector to the Vietnam War.

Mort, along with his busy practice, was the prosecutor for the town of Northvale, NJ, and represented school boards in Bergen County. He has been the recipient of numerous citations and awards for his legal skills, ethics and volunteerism.

Upon graduation from Boston University, Mort married Ida Betsy, a distant cousin of mine whose mother's family originated in Bayonne, NJ like my father's family. They had three children, Peter, a renowned biologist, Melissa, an attorney specializing in education and disability law, and Jeffrey, a Captain, and senior diver with the San Francisco Fire Department. Regretfully Ida Betsy passed away in her middle years, and after a while Mort married Marion a delightfully supportive person. They have a son Scott, a vice president at Meryll Lynch Wealth Management.

My life was greatly enhanced because of the many decades of association with Morton whom I could always depend on for great humor and good advise. We have traveled the road together for a longtime, summer and winter, up and down, and always together.

There have been other important people, in my life, whose presence has provided enjoyment whether I am with them, or thinking about them. Among them is SAUL FERN, a fraternity brother, who finished college before I even began, but has become a wonderful close friend when we discovered each other both living in New Jersey. Saul, recently attended the 72nd year class reunion of his high school graduation, from New London High School in Connecticut. Recently ZBT national fraternity honored Saul for his decades of leadership, philanthropy and humanitarianism.

ANGEL RIOS, retired international banker, great Saturday breakfast partner at the Stateline Diner, but who has moved to Sarasota, Florida so that our good times together are limited to texting, and occasional visits. MARGARET DUGGIN, my daughter's business associate until Covid ended the more than twenty years of *Yoga Haven*, Westchester County's most successful places for yoga. Margaret became a close family friend, and has completed her BSN and MSN, at Columbia University, after a field experience at a hospital in India.

⇢⇒ ⇐⇠

We all are better for being able to call DR. VICTORIA HOPE MADDEN our friend. No one is more caring, compassionate, or generous than Vicki Madden. After a long and successful career as Director of Science for the Paterson, NJ school district that includes over forty schools, Vicki guided the curriculum for the Meadowlands Environment Center, and directed a myriad of federal and state funded programs, originating from Ramapo College. Vicki, has travelled almost everywhere in the world, and shares her experiences with insight and great humor. Being with Vicki Madden is enlightening, and enjoyable for everyone fortunate enough to be her travel companions, on land and sea, and when regular travel in space becomes available, Vicki, will be there.

Our residing in Ramsey, NJ for over thirty years has allowed our family to participate in a wonderful social and caring community. The close friendship that developed between our family and PATTY and MARTY KOLB'S family that includes son Christopher, working in the data sales end of the financial world after his graduation from the University of Alabama, and daughter Kayla, who graduated from Rutgers last May. It has been joyful and delightful and at times when loss occurred, tragic, but the Kolbs, are always close by when sharing happiness or sorrow. Marty is an expert with anything mechanical or technical, and Patty is an accomplished "Wall Streeter." They are a wonderful couple, perfect and happy together.

We also have been fortunate to experience the kind and generous spirit of JOYCE (JAY) and STEVE HUDON, and their family who have enhanced our time in Ramsey by their friendship and devotion to the causes that assist those in need. Joyce and Steve, are delightful and engaging, and fun to be with. They have boundless energy, and are always seeking and working for good causes. Both the HUDONS, and the KOLBS are great examples of warm, supportive, and ethical families, in which children flourish, and become well-functioning adults.

Another longtime Ramsey friend is TONY IANNARELLI attorney and muckraker with a great independent spirit, who hiked the long Pacific Crest Trail just to have done it. Tony has written published editorials explaining that the Second Amendment never intended to allow everyone to own a gun, only members of, "A well ordered militia."

For nine years, I had the honor of assisting NANCY BOONE, while she was President of The Ramsey Historical Association. As the Vice President of the Association, I had the good fortune to help remake a moribund organization into a modern, vital, active group of residents passionate about their town's history. NANCY BOONE who was born and raised in Ramsey singlehandedly created the most well known, and longest running Farmer's Market in our entire region. Every Sunday dozens of selected vendors of produce, and specialty foods gather at the giant local railroad station parking lot to offer fine products to the several hundred attendees.

Chapter 7

"The Most Interesting Man in the World"

ONE MORNING, OVER ten years ago I received a telephone call from my longtime friend from our first day at Boston University. It was MORTON COVITZ with whom I have been close to for decades.

On the day he called, Morton asked, "Who is the most interesting man in the world?" I responded, "You are of course." That was not what he meant, at that time anyway. He said, "It's Jon Lippe." That shocked me. Morton was referring to the iconic personality seen in the commercials on all television stations, and especially on ESPN, the Dos Equis beer's international symbol, "The Most Interesting Man in the World."

The actor representing Dos Equis, and selling more of their product than was ever imagined was a mature, debonair, handsome, Spanish sounding, and appearing man. Morton, was claiming that the Dos Equis man was our fraternity brother, and my college roommate Jon Lippe, now known as JONATHAN GOLDSMITH.

I did some research on Google, and to my great surprise Jon Lippe was indeed Jonathan Goldsmith, "The Most Interesting Man in the World." I found online the February 7, 2011 article titled *Interesting* written by Nick Paumgarten for *New Yorker* magazine complete with a great big pen and ink sketch of Jonathan Goldsmith. The article begins with "The most interesting thing about the man who plays the Most Interesting Man in the World, in those TV ads for Dos Equis beer is that he is interesting too."

Yes, he always was interesting, mysterious, and relentlessly sure of himself. I actually first got to know him, when we were about nine years old, and he spent the summer with relatives who lived across the street from my house in Long Beach, NY, and he was called Jono Lippe. We played together every day, and it was a great summer, for both of us. When his mom arrived to pick Jono up at the summer's end it was obvious he was not happy about leaving to return home to Mt. Kisco in Westchester County. Greta, his mother, was strikingly beautiful, which even at my young age, I realized. She was a Conover model, which at the time was one of the two leading model agencies in New York, and therefore in the entire country. Jono's parents were divorced, and he lived with his mother, and her wealthy husband. His father, Milton Goldsmith with whom Jonathan was always close was a physical education teacher at James Monroe High School, in the Bronx, and a semi-professional basketball player. After that summer, I didn't see Jono again until he showed up at Boston University a year after I started there. We became fraternity brothers, and then roommates for a year, in an apartment on Buswell Street in Brookline two blocks from the university's main campus, and four blocks from Fenway Park.

Sometime after college Jon Lippe, legally changed his name back to Johnathan Goldsmith, and enrolled in acting classes at the, Living Theatre, in New York City, along with future stars Dustin Hoffman, with whom he didn't get along, and Robert Duvall. After a stint at The Neighborhood Playhouse School of the Theater honing his acting

Faces from a Good Life

skills, Goldsmith eventually moved to Los Angeles, and began making the rounds of auditions for any role he could play on television or in films. Jonathan Goldsmith became known as the guy who gets killed on almost every popular crime show. His credits include roles on *Bonanza, Hawaii Five-O, The Rockford Files, Mannix, Barnaby Jones, Gunsmoke, T.J. Hooker, MacGyver, CHIPS, Knots Landing, Magnum, PI, Charlie's Angels, Perry Mason, Dynasty, The Streets of San Francisco and Dallas.* He had featured roles in several movies, and supporting roles, in about twenty-five Westerns, but couldn't capture a leading part in a TV series even with the influence of his closest friend movie star, Fernando Lamas. Lamas was married to Esther Williams the glamorous swimming star of countless movies. They often invited Goldsmith to their home, and to accompany them to events and social occasions. In addition to Fernando Lamas, whom Goldsmith called Fern he also was mentored by his good friends, screen legends Shelly Winters, Joan Fontaine, and Elaine Stritch who all tried to help his career, but weren't successful.

Jonathan Goldman's life in Hollywood was anything but boring. In his autobiographical book *Stay Interesting* published in 2017, Goldsmith, provides the details of a swirl of love affairs, one-night stands and even more casual sexual experiences during several decades in Hollywood. I have to admit that if I had been the writer helping Jonathan with his story or his editor at Dutton, I would have insisted on a much more conservative approach to the telling of his admittedly fascinating life story. His long list of dalliances, some identified, most not by name is dizzying as was his ability to attract lovely young women during his undergraduate days. Often I would come back to our apartment, from class in the afternoon, and discover Jon's latest girlfriend, whom he hadn't known that morning, in our bathroom dressing and brushing her hair.

Ron Kase

One of Jonathan Goldsmith's best stories as outlined in his book *Stay Interesting* was the time he secured a role on the famous series *Gunsmoke*, which was viewed on television for twenty years of original programs, and is still seen as reruns. He was selected, without auditioning, for a featured role on the Western series. Later on he also played a dozen different roles in the same series over the total run of *Gunsmoke*. When hired for the first time by well-known television director Marc Daniels, (*I Love Lucy, Where's Raymond, The Golden Girls*) Jonathan was asked by the director, "You know how to ride a horse son?" "Like the wind sir," was Goldsmith's answer. Of course, growing up in the Bronx he didn't know how to ride a horse, had practically never seen a horse. Eventually, after lots of pain, he did learn to ride, and was in every popular Western series of the day, and many movies of the same genre. He said he may hold the record for falling off more horses than anyone else in Hollywood.

At one point the roles in the Westerns dry up even after co-starring with Bert Lancaster, John Wayne, and Joseph Cotton the work becomes elusive. However, he always survives in Los Angles even broke, homeless, and living in his pickup truck Goldsmith gets by. Any kind of work in and out of show business is accepted, and he maintains his close relationship with his father back in the Bronx. He does have success in a business, and has to give it up, but it allows him to live on a sixty-foot sailboat in Marina del Rey. He's an experienced sailor, as well as a mountain climber, and an environmentalist. He admits he's "A hustler, a good hustler." That's how he gets along in Hollywood once the acting jobs stopped, he believed forever, but Barbara his agent, never lost faith in Jonathan Goldsmith.

In 2005, Heineken, the international beer company, and owner of the Dos Equis brand, decided to find a spokesman, who through a unique campaign would drastically increase sales of the Mexican beer, in the U.S. market. But they were seeking a different sort of spokesman, doing something never tried before in television advertising. The company's advertising agency, suggested they look for a sophisticated, obviously Hispanic man with a slight accent, and a commanding voice. Jonathan's agent Barbara, pushed him to audition for the role, in the Dos Equis commercial. He however believed he was wrong for the part, but nevertheless Goldsmith showed up at the studio where the auditions were taking place. His greatest concern that day however wasn't about the audition, but parking his old pickup truck in the street at a meter nearby, would he get a ticket once the paid time had elapsed, and even worse, would the truck be towed? As he approached the studio building, he saw a large crowd that he estimated at five hundred men all younger than him, all Hispanic, and all auditioning for the Dos Equis commercial.

Jonathan Goldsmith tells the following story. After a long wait, he's called in for the audition in a dark studio with only one chair that is illuminated by a spot light. There's a video camera on the wall amid a bank of recording equipment to record his answers, and reactions to the questions fed to him by the director, the agency people, and the client back in New York. Goldsmith seemed to have an epiphany, and suddenly realized that the part was the role he had been preparing for his entire professional life. He begins by speaking with a Spanish accent borrowed from his good friend Fernando Lamas. He tells stories, and the more outrageous they are he is received with laughter and encouragement from the group in New York. As he talks about arm wrestling Fidel Castro, Goldsmith adds using the great accent that he also had sex with Che Guevara's sister after lending Che his motorcycle. The team members in New York were laughing hysterically, and Jonathan became worried again about his truck parked, at an expired parking meter.

After the audition the truck was still there, and without a ticket. He called Barbara his agent, and told her he was wrong for the part, and she shouldn't waste her time on it. Six weeks passed, and Goldsmith forgot about the Dos Equis commercial, until the day he was called back for another audition. That day after the producers had scoured South America, and Mexico there were about one hundred new actors, young and Hispanic, as competition. But, Jonathan came through and obviously had another great performance. After another two months of waiting, he received a call for a third audition. This time there were only two other actors, and the three of them did auditions in full makeup and wardrobe. Goldsmith, was even more confident and gave the performance of a lifetime. The next day, after his agent had to convince the casting director that only an older person could logically have had the experiences that will be featured in the commercials, Jonathan Goldsmith became "The Most Interesting Man in the World."

The role lased about a dozen years. An amazing run for a product's spokesman. Goldsmith, became internationally famous. His face and wise words were immortalized, and the series of commercials seen all the time on every TV channel became a cult classic. My associate at the college, the extraordinary grant writer, and the best baker of apple pies CLAUDIA ESKER and her friends in Boonton, NJ were "Most Interesting Man" groupies, and acquired from a liquor store a life size cardboard cutout of Jonathan Goldsmith, in his role holding a bottle of Dos Equis. They brought it to all of the neighborhood parties. I arranged for each of them to receive a personalized autographed picture of the "Most Interesting Man."

After Morton Covitz's phone call, I sent a letter to Jonathan. He promptly answered my letter. I told him I discovered he was the Dos Equis spokesman. We talked on the phone a few times, catching up on all the years, since we were roommates at Boston University. He and Barbara his agent had married, after divorcing their spouses, and they lived on his sailboat, in Marina del Rey for a while. They moved to Vermont as his fame and fortune grew. He spoke about the other famous people who approached him to compliment his performance in the commercials. To name only a few they included Michael Jordon, Warren Beatty, and Leonardo DiCaprio and his most unbelievable, but documented meeting was with President Barack Obama at Camp David. Jonathan, and I communicate by email. He travels a lot to raise funds for the organization that actually removes buried land mines in Cambodia, and other places in Southeast Asia where war has left the deadly explosives that are still killing innocent people. He's a leader of the Democratic Party in Vermont, and during the vulgar Trump presidency Jonathan, and I regularly exchanged information regarding Trump's latest crimes, and other offences.

One evening Jonathan and I had dinner in Manhattan, at a restaurant on Avenue of the Americas (6th Avenue) across from Rockefeller Center. As we followed the maître d to our table other diners recognized him, and smiled or waved. I commented that I felt good to be with the, "Most Interesting Man in the World." He corrected me by saying, I was with the, "Luckiest Man in the World."

CHAPTER 8

My Uncle Max

MY UNCLE MAX, was actually my father's first cousin. He was two years older than my dad, so Max was Uncle Max to me. His father Solomon, was the brother of my grandfather Soel, and apparently, they immigrated together to the United States, in the late 1880s. Max was born in 1897, on Manhattan's Lower East Side, amidst the Jewish life of over-crowded tenements, street peddlers, and sweatshops. He had five siblings, and at times they were placed with relatives when the family didn't have enough money to feed everyone.

It's likely that Max didn't finish high school because he began full time work at sixteen, as an office boy for the daily newspaper, *The New York Evening Mail*. He stayed at the newspaper for almost four years learning everything he could about news editing, production and reporting. In 1917, he became a staff member of the Hearst newspapers' wire service, the *International News Service* (INS) that provided stories, photos, and copy for other newspapers throughout the United States. Max Kase's bylined stories covering financial markets, and corporate mergers, which were mysterious to almost all news readers at the time. They were well received by other big city, and also rural newspapers that carried the INS stories, with Max's name on the top. Max remained with the Hearst Newspaper organization until 1966, when the *New*

Ron Kase

York Journal-American went out of business, and he retired after a career spanning forty-nine years.

By 1922 Max began to write feature stories, the highest level of newspaper writing. He wrote about the motion picture industry, and the attempt to have it return to New York from scandalous Hollywood, by a scheme to build a great new movie production center on Long Island. He wrote about the Jazz Age, and flappers, and readers loved the stories. Somehow this man with limited formal education, from a poor immigrant led family became a sophisticated, erudite and prolific writer, whose work was enjoyed by thousands of readers every day.

Always interested in whatever professional sports that were available to observe, Max, began to write about boxing in 1923. Jack Dempsey the heavy weight champion, agreed to fight Luis Firpo, "The Wild Bull of the Pampas." Max, stayed at Dempsey's training camp in upstate New York, and wrote daily stories about the champ. People were actually quite interested in the reports, and newspapers from all over picked up Max's stories. His last report from Dempsey's training camp was kind of melancholy.

> "The hotel which was thronged for more than a month with tin-eared prize fighters, trainers, rubbers, and dozens of reporters, scores of vacationalists, and tourists, now is silent and deserted. The lobbies which were jammed and crowded now echo hollowly with footsteps of a forlorn bartender, a sad hearted innkeeper and an occasional waiter."
> September 13, 1923, Indiana Evening Gazette

Max, and Dempsey, remained friends for the rest of their lives. Jack Dempsey's restaurant on Broadway, in Manhattan, was a famous tourist spot that was known for porterhouse steaks and roast beef sandwiches. Max was often a guest there when Dempsey was in town, and at his restaurant. Max wrote about other prize fighters, and became identified with the sport that was so popular sixty thousand spectators turned out for a lightweight championship fight in Yankee Stadium between Benny Leonard, and Lew Tendler. Leonard who began life in the same Lower East Side Jewish neighborhood as Max Kase, won and became world champion. Max dubbed him "The Old Master."

On a Saturday in the 1950s, Max showed up at our home in Long Beach, NY with boxers Rocky Marciano who was the heavy weight champion, and Jake LaMotta the former middle weight champion. My Uncle Moe and Aunt Helen, were also there. Moe was my father's older brother, and the most successful in business. He and Max were close having spent the most time together growing up. Max and the fighters had stopped off at the local kosher style delicatessen, and bought many pounds of corned beef, pastrami, salami, dill pickles and rye bread, to bring to our home. They had been at the Sunnyside Gardens Arena, in Long Island City, a famous training ground for up and coming boxers, and decided to visit with us. It was a great evening, odd but nice. A few of our neighbors dropped in to meet the famous fighters.

William Randolph Hearst during his adult life was one of America's richest, and most powerful individuals due to his owning newspapers, in every section of the country, as well as magazines, radio stations, and the movies he produced, primarily for his mistress of thirty years Marion Davies. He was also a politician, and is credited with forcing the United States into the Spanish-American War of 1898 that relieved Cuba from cruel Spanish rule, and ceded Puerto Rico, the Philippines, and Guam to the United States. Hearst, built his estate known as "Hearst Castle," in San Simeon, California, on two hundred and forty

Ron Kase

thousand acres, which housed his enormous art, antiques, Greek vases, and silver collections that after his death were given, along with the castle to the State of California for a museum open to the public.

Hearst actually noticed the good quality of Max Kase's writing, and in 1924, Hearst appointed him editor and General Manager of *The Havana Telegram,* and Max moved to Havana, Cuba where he stayed for two years. This event in Max's life is especially interesting to me because of our times in Cuba during the years when we could offer travelers excursions to the island country through Bestkase Travel, LLC. It was some of the most exciting and interesting travel I have ever undertaken. While there, I remembered that Uncle Max had been a newspaper editor in Havana, which made our times in Cuba more compelling, since I had to wonder how he had been able to function so well in the always turbulent Cuban culture.

Max returned to New York as a sports writer for Hearst's *New York Journal* a morning newspaper. He began to cover National League baseball, and continued to cover boxing for Hearst Newspapers throughout the country. Always a loyal employee of the Hearst Empire, Max next went to Boston in 1934 as sports editor of the *Boston American,,* and during his time in Boston, Max developed a friendship with Walter A. Brown, the owner of the Boston Celtics basketball team, and president of the Boston Garden. Their association was the spark that later on led to Max's role in founding the present day NBA. He was convinced that professional basketball could be a national success. Basketball was played professionally primarily in the Midwest, and was generally ignored by sports writers. Max, left Boston in 1936, and returned to New York City as a reporter and columnist for the newly combined, *New York Journal-American,* becoming the sports editor two years later, a position he held for twenty-eight years.

Along with being the sports editor for the newspaper, Max, wrote a daily column on sports titled, *Brief Kase*. He continued to cover baseball, but now followed the New York Yankees, and the American League, for all the Hearst papers. *Brief Kase,* was also reprinted in the *Sporting News* a popular afternoon newspaper that primarily covered horse racing. In 1937 Max became part of the eight member committee of baseball writers that chose the American League's Most Valuable Player an annual award. Max Kase was a fixture in the New York sporting world from the 1930s to the 1960s. Charley Rosen, in his book, *The First Tipoff, The Incredible Story of the Birth of the NBA* describes and records the legend of Max Kase.

> **"During his career, his trademark widow's peak and devilish smile were seen at every conceivable sporting event from basketball to baseball, from football to ice hockey, from rodeos to bullfights, from six-day bicycle races to flagpole-sitting contests, as well as boxing and wrestling matches, dog shows, and track meets. Along the way, he'd meet and befriend everybody who was worth knowing."**

During World War II, Max was responsible for the sale of millions of dollars of War Bonds, issued by the United States Government to finance our role in the war. He became the chairman of the Fifth War Loan Sports Committee that sold an additional almost seventeen million dollars in bonds for the war, by organizing sporting events in New York City. They included a War Bond Day at Aqueduct Racetrack, a golf exhibition, a sports carnival at the Polo Grounds, and an unusual three-way baseball game that included all three of the New York teams, also held at the Polo Grounds, the home of the New York Giants baseball and football teams. The stadium was located in upper Manhattan, above Central Park between 111th and 112th Streets. It was the home of the New York Giants Baseball team, until they moved to San Francisco, California in 1957. The New York Giants football team played in the Polo Grounds for thirty years, before relocating to the New Jersey Meadowlands. The stadium was demolished in 1964.

In 1945, at age forty-eight Max Kase married Katy Gallagher a pretty blond shiksa about six years younger. Katy was a delightful companion to Max who was well known and always being invited to celebrations and events in New York City. She was smart, stylish and a great conversationalist, and all the men in our family were envious, and the women jealous of Katy's good looks and charming manner. After residing for a while in Max's large apartment in Brooklyn's Flatbush section, they purchased a home on Hawley Place in Yonkers, NY. Hawley Place was a short street high up on the Yonkers' Palisades. The house had a wonderful view of the Hudson River about two hundred feet below. In fact, Max and Katy loved their home's location so much they bought the house next to theirs, when it came up for sale, and rented it to a writer and his family. Max and Katy's home was less than a tenth of a mile from Seton College, and before my time there Katy was a volunteer in the college's library for several years, and made friends with all of the. Sisters of Charity on the campus.

A bachelor party was held for Max at *Toots Shor's* restaurant, on West 51st just off of 5th Avenue. Somewhere, I have a photograph of my father at the party standing, smoking a cigar and applauding someone, or something being said about Max. The hundred or so close friends and relatives enjoyed being at the famous New York restaurant where celebrities that included Joe DiMaggio, Jackie Gleason, Frank Sinatra, Marilyn Monroe and even Ernest Hemingway, were seen when they were in town. Bernard "Toots" Shor attended high school with my father, in Bayonne, NJ. Toots was a crude bombastic individual, sort of an early model for Elaine Kaufman, owner of *Elaine's* to emulate decades later. No one went to Toots Shor's for the food, which was average at best, but to see who was there, and be seen. Jimmy Walker the flamboyant former mayor of New York City known as "Beau James" was master of ceremonies at Max's bachelor party.

At about the same time as Max and Katy's nuptials, Max, began to seriously look into forming a professional basketball league with teams playing in the major cities. Max and Walter A. Brown, owner of the Boston Celtics agreed to work together to establish the league. Max Kase organized a basketball exhibition in New York featuring two top touring basketball teams. An overflow crowd turned out for charity event held at Madison Square Garden, which was located on 8th Avenue between 49th and 50th Streets. The Garden was there from 1925 to 1968, and then moved to its present location above Pennsylvania Station on 33rd Street. The impressive turn out for the exhibition basketball game convinced Max that there would be a strong following for a professional team in New York. Max intended to own, and be the General Manager of the New York franchise to be called the Knickerbockers, now known as the New York Knicks.

Max approached the president of the Madison Square Garden Corporation Ned Ireland, who had promoted college basketball successfully at the arena. Max's plan was to lease the venue, on open dates, for the new professional basketball league he was organizing. Ireland, claimed that the agreement among all major arenas in the country, allowed only professional teams owned by the arena's management to use the facilities. Walter A. Brown, president of the Boston Garden wasn't aware of this rule, but Ned Ireland refused to allow a basketball team owned by Max Kase to play in Madison Square Garden. Ireland, on his own recruited and established the original New York Knicks basketball team. Max sued and Ireland settled out of court. No one knows the amount paid to Max, but hopefully it was enough to purchase the house next to his on Hawley Place. Max's role in the origination of the National Basketball Association (NBA) is well documented.

"The Basketball Association of America that became the NBA, a bastard child, sprang from the unlikely parentage of pro hockey and the Hearst press. Max Kase, sports editor of Hearst's New York Journal-American, conceived the national association and drew up its charter...Kase's idea was to fill those empty dates with pro basketball." Big Leagues Professional Baseball, Football and Basketball in National Memory. Stephen Fox, University of Nebraska Press

Walter Kennedy, commissioner of the NBA from 1963 to 1975, said, "Kase's personal involvement in the beginning of the NBA... and his strong belief that pro basketball was destined to be a major sport were important factors in the growth and success of the NBA," Bangor Daily News (AP story)

"Led by Walter Brown of Boston and Max Kase of New York (and the New York Journal-American) the arena operators ended up forming a league that had teams in 11 major cities..." Basketball: The American Game. Joe Jares, Follett Publishing.

Max's love of basketball stayed with him even after being pushed out of the NBA. He and the *Journal-American* sports reporters were carefully following up on rumors, and actual charges that college basketball players were shaving points in games that were heavily bet on, through illegal bookmakers. The players were accused of having received cash payments from the gamblers who were making large profits, due to their knowing that the basketball game's scores, and the point spreads were being controlled by the players. In January 1951, Max met with Manhattan District Attorney Frank Hogan the famous incorruptible prosecutor who set the standard for the DA's office that is followed to this day. Max shared his findings with Frank Hogan, who developed a solid case proving that players from colleges in New York, Kentucky, and Illinois were working hand in hand with bookmakers. After the case became public, Max wrote a series of articles describing the bribery and corruption, and castigated the participants as being "disloyal" to their colleges, and for "calloused greed."

In 1952, Max Kase was awarded a Pulitzer Prize for exposing the college basketball scandal, and for his articles published in the *New York Journal American*. The citation read, "For his exclusive exposures of bribery and other items of corruption, in the popular American sport of basketball, which exposures tended to restore confidence in the game's integrity." A testimonial dinner in celebration of Max's extraordinary achievement of being awarded the Pulitzer Prize was held at Toot's Shor's Restaurant, and attended by two hundred of the leading figures in sports, the press, and New York politicians. District Attorney Frank Hogan, paid tribute to Max at the dinner. "I humbly and contritely express my appreciation for what Max Kase did. This was the act of a person conscious of the welfare of the community."

The Hearst Sandlot Baseball Classic, was conceived by Max Kase in 1946, and it continued to 1965. Young men, age sixteen to eighteen, were selected for the national all-star team from players in twelve cities where Hearst newspapers were published. The players came to New York City, and played a series against the New York all-star team, selected by the sports reporters of the *New York Journal-American*. The Classic was played in the Polo Grounds until 1959, and then at Yankee Stadium. Max convinced his good friend Babe Ruth to serve as chairman of the Hearst Sandlot Classic, which over the twenty years of games played, produced eighty-eight players who went on to play major league baseball. Max and the Babe were confidants, and spent a good deal of time together on vacations, after the Babe retired from baseball. On a table in Max's living room, an 5x7 autographed photo of Babe Ruth stood for as long as I can remember. I always admired the photo, and Max, offered it to me, when I was eight or nine years old, but my mother of course, wouldn't allow it. The Babe died in 1948, and his honorary pall bearers were Joe DiMaggio, Connie Mack, owner of the Philadelphia Athletics baseball team, and Max Kase.

Just like the rest of the Kase family, Max was culturally Jewish, but not at all religious. However, in 1950 Max was the founder of the New York Sports Lodge of B'nai B'rith, a Jewish organization that supported the Anti-Defamation League's campaign against religious intolerance that is more active than ever today. He was president for two terms. My father and uncles were charter members, and in 1975 the organization was renamed the Max Kase Sports Lodge.

After retiring, Max kept busy writing articles for the *Taxi News* and *The Sporting News*. Then to everyone's surprise he opened two restaurants in Manhattan called Brief Kase, one located at the Port Authority Bus Terminal, and the other close to Madison Square Garden. As far as I know, the restaurants were the first "Sports Bars" anywhere in the country. I admit that I hadn't visited either place so I don't know if they were successful, or how long they stayed open. Max and Katy, weren't cooks, and they ate in restaurants almost daily, so owning two made sense. They were married for twenty-nine years. Max passed away in 1974 from a heart attack, after having an amazing career, caring friends and a happy marriage.

CHAPTER 9

The Irish Connection

"We have always found the Irish a bit odd.
They refuse to be English-----"
Winston Churchill

"Being Irish, he had an abiding sense of tragedy, which sustained him through temporary periods of joy."
William Butler Yates

"I'm convinced, the Irish having many of the same peculiarities as the Jews, are one of the lost tribes of Israel."
Gustave Kase

MY FIRST TRIP to Ireland took place about twenty-five years ago. Jonathan was four, and already a seasoned traveler. Kathleen packed lots of heavy sweaters for our springtime visit to the Old Sod. However, upon arriving at Shannon Airport in the morning, we discovered the temperature outside to be in the eighties, and it remained warm for our ten-day visit. We purchased summer clothing, and didn't unpack the heavy sweaters. Kathleen Foley Kase is part of an Irish-American family of six siblings all born in Irvington-on-Hudson, NY, and whose parents, Jack (John E.) and Marilyn (Murphy) Foley, were also natives of Westchester County that is located just north of New York City. During our several visits to Ireland, I would kiddingly mention to Kathleen that she was the only Irish-American who didn't have relatives currently living in Ireland. The reason for that is her ancestors began emigrating early in the 19th Century, and apparently to a single location; the eastern bank of the Hudson River, running north from Yonkers to Tarrytown. While the Foley and Murphy clans can be traced back several generations in Ireland, there was great impetus to leave the troubled land beset with the cruelty of British rule, poverty, famine, and civil war.

Kathleen's sister, Maureen Marshall, had painstakingly researched their family's history, and as one hopes for, discovered forgotten ancestors born in Westmeath County, in the center of Ireland. Third great grandparents Patrick Murray, and Ann Doyle, both born in 1795 produced a daughter Mary Murray born in 1830, who married John Duff, born in 1826 both in Westmeath County. What is significant is that Mary and John, Kathleen's great, great grandparents, immigrated, and found their way to Irvington, NY, where Mary lived until 1885, and John until 1886. Their daughter Margaret, born in 1855 in Irvington married, Michael Kiernan born in Trim, County Meath to the north of Dublin. The Foley name emerges when John Foley, born in Ireland in 1831 marries Brigid Quinn born 1830 also in Ireland. They immigrated and resided in Tarrytown, NY, Brigid until dying in 1892, and John, in 1912. Son JJ Foley, born in 1863 in Tarrytown, NY married Anna Wynne, born in 1865 in Williamstown, Galway County, in western Ireland. They also took up residence in Irvington, NY, for the rest of their lives. JJ died in 1934, Anna, in 1950. Their son was Edward J. Foley the beloved grandfather of Kathleen and her siblings.

The Kiernan ancestors hastily left Ireland one dark rainy night to seek safety in America because of an incident involving Patrick Kiernan, Michael's brother. Patrick was in-route to his home from downtown Trim and as he crossed the bridge spanning the Boyne River, he met an approaching British soldier. The soldier, ordered Patrick to step off the narrow sidewalk into the gutter to allow him to pass. Patrick picked up the soldier and flung him head first into the river below. The soldier drowned, and the British garrison began a house-to-house search for Patrick. That night, the family hastily fled to America. Visiting Trim, in August, 2022, two decedents of the Kiernans my wife Kathleen, and our son Jonathan stood on the same bridge almost two centuries later. Jonathan threw an expired Bank of England five-pound note into the water to commemorate his ancestor's flight from British tyranny.

Edward J. Foley was born in Tarrytown in 1901, and died in Irvington in 1987. He was a sergeant with the Irvington Police Department for twenty years. A photograph of Sergeant Foley, on his Indian police department motorcycle is in a prominent place, in our home's family room. Also fascinating, Kathleen's brother Michael is the current Sergeant Foley with the Irvington Police Department. Grandpa Edward married Mary Agnes McGovern, also born in 1901 in Irvington, and died there in 1998. She was a close and loved grandmother of Kathleen and her brothers and sisters: Maureen, Eileen, John, Michael and Patrick. Edward, known as Tuck, and Mary, known as Tiny had a son John (Jack) E. Foley, father to Kathleen and her five siblings, and a daughter Agnes married to Kevin O'Neil, mayor of Irvington for multiple terms, and later highway commissioner for the Township of Greenburg. The O'Neils had four children.

The Murphy side of Kathleen's family also has a history of Irish immigrants arriving in the river towns of Westchester County in the 19th

Century. Great, great grandparents were John Laffan, born in Ireland in 1832, and died in East Irvington in 1901 and Ellen Laffan also born in Ireland in 1841, who died in 1897 in East Irvington. Their daughter Johanna, (1864-1931) married, William G. Murphy (1863-1894). They resided in Tarrytown close by to East Irvington. The section of private homes located between Irvington-on-Hudson, and Tarrytown called East Irvington, was known as "Dublin" because of the preponderance of Irish Americans living there. At the present time, the New York State Thruway divides Tarrytown and East Irvington, and the entire area has become multi-cultural.

Beloved Murphy grandparents were Frank, and Mary Murphy. Frank P. Murphy was born in Hastings-on-Hudson, another river town in 1891, and died in 1970. He married Mary Natalie O'Donnell from Yonkers born in 1901, and died in Irvington in 1985. Their daughter Marilyn born in 1929 married John E. Foley, and they became the parents of Kathleen, and her five siblings.

Grandpa Frank served in the U.S. Army during World War I. He was a corporal with the 9th Machine-Gun Battalion notably in the battle of Chateau Thierry in France, a turning point of the war. Frank Murphy was awarded the Distinguished Service Cross for consistent bravery fighting the enemy, and while wounded himself he cared for the other wounded men in his company. The battalion was under the command of General John J. Pershing known as Black Jack Pershing, due to his former command in 1895 of the 10th Calvary of African American troops known as "Buffalo Soldiers." A framed photograph of the entire company showing Grandpa Frank, in the first row, along with General Pershing is a treasured memento that has hung in our breakfast room for decades. Frank was a tree surgeon, and the family lived in an elegant Victorian home on Neperan Road in Tarrytown prior to moving to Irvington. Over two decades ago, when the house was on the market, Kathleen, Marilyn and I during an afternoon drive visited the former Murphy family home high up on the Tarrytown hills. *(Letters from Frank Murphy sent from France during World War I are at the end of this chapter.)*

Marilyn had three brothers; Tom, Frank and Jay. Tom, was a New York City school teacher, and his daughter, Dr. Laura Murphy is a distinguished historian who has researched, and recorded the role of Catholic women and labor priests, in the development of minimum wage laws, in the United States. Laura received a dissertation fellowship from the Cushwa Center for the Study of American Catholicism at Notre Dame University. She received her Ph.D. from Binghamton University of SUNY, and her undergraduate degree from the University of Memphis, in the city where she resided for eight years. Presently, Laura is professor of history, and chairperson of the History, Government and Economics department, at SUNY Dutchess Community College in Poughkeepsie, NY. Due to her extensive background in music, along with having a fine contralto voice, Laura sings with the band *The Vague Assurances* whose music we enjoy whenever we attend one of the band's concerts. Laura lives in an historic section of Poughkeepsie, NY in a charming home with writer and professor of American literature, Dr. Keith O'Neill.

Triple Great Grandfather Thomas F. Curran was born in 1848 in Yonkers, and was a Drummer Boy in the United States Civil War, a member of the 35th New Jersey Infantry a terrible responsibility for a young man. He lived until 1896, and years later his family contributed the Civil War drum to the Tarrytown Historical Society. The Drummer Boys were an important part of the military strategy at the time of the Civil War. Communications between commanders and troops were limited so drummer boys provided the signals by drumming loudly to assemble, advance, retreat, and signal other commands. The Drummer Boys also assisted the army surgeons, were stretcher bearers and helped to bury the fallen soldiers. They witnessed the worst parts of the nation's most destructive war.

Thomas F. Curran married, Mary Ann Mulligan. Their daughter Margaret born in Yonkers in 1874 later married Patrick Francis O'Donnell, also a Yonkers resident born in 1875. Their son James J. O'Donnell was a distinguished attorney in Yonkers. He was a graduate of New York University, and earned a law degree at Fordham University. James, was a prominent Republican Party leader at the time when Republicans were good loyal Americans. He was also a naval officer during World War II. I knew his law partner, William F. Condon when I was a director of the anti-poverty program in lower Westchester, and Bill Condon was a member of the board of trustees. James O'Donnell, died in 1972 at age 65, under suspicious circumstances leaving his wife Ann Mooney, and three children.

There is a notable fact connected with the origins in America of both the Foley and Murphy families which, of course, originated in Ireland many generations ago. Upon their immigrating, separately or as couples or families, both sides somehow avoided the ugly, over crowded, poverty life of New York City's lower East Side, and Boston's South End. Both cities were the major receiving centers for Irish citizens emigrating from the middle of the 1800s to early in the 20th Century. Apparently Foley, ancestors found employment on the baronial estates in Irving-on-Hudson, and similar properties close by in Tarrytown. The area attracted the wealthy of the Golden Age who constructed mansions on large estates mostly overlooking the Hudson River.

Faces from a Good Life

A north/south road built during Colonial times was the Queen's Highway later known as the Albany Post Road (Route 9), since it ran between Manhattan and Albany, NY. The road became Broadway, and rendered the river towns in Westchester easily accessible for wealthy families who desired to get away from the pollution found at the time in Manhattan. Others in their socioeconomic group built actual castles further north along the Hudson because they were reminded of castles on the Rhine River in Europe.

The estates of Irvington included "Nevis," built on two hundred and three acres by James Hamilton son of Alexander Hamilton, who named the property after the Caribbean Island where his father was born. The estate was acquired by the du Pont family of Delaware in 1920, and later Alice du Pont donated the property to Columbia University for the establishment of a center for Advanced Scientific Research in physics. Ironically, Col. James Hamilton was a graduate of Columbia University.

Early American author Washington Irving built his charming home "Sunnyside" in 1835 on twenty-four acres that are still intact and open for visitors. Francis Cottnet a French importer of cloth bought one hundred acres above the river in 1852, and built "Nuits," his grand estate that featured an Italian Villa style mansion. The inventor of the telegraph cable Cyrus West Field acquired five hundred acres for an enormous estate called "Ardsley" after his ancestor's home in England. Field put down the first telegraph cable on the floor of the Atlantic Ocean, and after four attempts successfully linked America to England. John McVicker's estate in Irvington contained one hundred acres with a fanciful mansion, and there were others.

In Tarrytown's "Millionaires Colony," John D. Rockefeller bought three thousand four hundred acres in 1893, and built "Kykuit" (lookout) on the highest spot in Westchester County. The mansion is a forty room stone Georgian Classical Revival style house that three generations of Rockefellers occupied until gifting it to the public as a museum. Just prior to the building of Kykuit, the brother of John D., William Rockefeller built "Rockwood Hall a two hundred and four room mansion directly on the Hudson River, the present site of Phelps Memorial Hospital. In 1890 Julian Detmar, built his castle on twenty-seven acres in Tarrytown, and General William Howard Carroll lived in "Carrollcliffe," the castle he had constructed in 1897. The grandest house in Tarrytown was "Lyndhurst" the home of railroad magnate and financier Jay Gould. The mansion was built on a sixty-seven-acre estate overlooking the Hudson River, in the Gothic Revival style. Lyndhurst is the best example of Golden Age architecture, and its *Robber Baron* reputation, and is presently open to the public as a National Historic Site. Also in Tarrytown Robert Hoe a founder of the Metropolitan Museum of Art, and owner of a *Gutenberg Bible,* lived in "Maplehurst." "Hillcrest" was the home of Mark Twain, for just two years before the famous writer moved to Hartford, Connecticut. The mansion became the popular "Tappan Hill."

The owners of the grand homes and estates needed experienced people to tend to the family's life when they occupied the houses, and to keep the gardens and lawns, in pristine condition. Some of the properties housed horse stables along with barns for cows and sheep that required care. Luckily for the Irish who immigrated to the eastern hills of the Hudson River, there was plenty of work available in much more pleasant surroundings than the unhealthy and often dangerous sweat shops of New York City.

Kathleen's parents, Jack and Marilyn Murphy Foley were active residents of Irvington for their entire adult lives. Marilyn, graduated from

SUNY College at New Paltz with a degree in education, and certification to teach in New York. Marilyn taught reading in the White Plains, NY public schools. She also taught in their parish school, and was well known for always assisting anyone in need. For about twenty-five years, Marilyn was an active leader of the Irvington Girl Scouts long after Kathleen and her sisters had left scouting. For several years, she directed a program, funded by the New York State Education Department that reached hundreds of underserved high school students in Yonkers. They were introduced to a variety of cultural events, and experiences designed to encourage a commitment to attend college. The program was sponsored by Seton College.

Jack had a fine lifelong career with Con Edison where he specialized in customer relations. He was the fire chief of Irvington for many years, and Kathleen remembers the nights he was summoned out due to fires or deadly car crashes on the nearby Saw Mill River Parkway, and then would go to the Con Edison office, in the morning. He was a good kind man, a pillar of the Irvington community known and respected by everyone. Regretfully, he passed away without any warning at age sixty-five a year after Kathleen and I married. Jack's funeral mass in Irvington was celebrated by our dear friend Father Neil O'Connell. The funeral cortege bringing Jack Foley from Immaculate Conception Church in Irvington, to the historic Sleepy Hollow Cemetery in North Tarrytown was a mile long befitting a man who had a life of service to others.

Marilyn Murphy Foley wife of Jack, mother of six, grandmother, educator and community leader was a delightful person to be with anywhere at any time. I considered Marilyn my good friend, and she also was my mother-in-law. Marilyn, was only ten years older than me so we had mutual knowledge of the times. I thoroughly enjoyed our conversations, and will always miss her. After Kathleen, and I married, Marilyn, began to visit my mother who resided in a long-term care facility, in Nanuet, NY. I didn't ask Marilyn to do that great deed, she just said it was the right thing to do. My mother always appreciated Marilyn's visits as did I. Soon after Jonathan was born Marilyn began to suffer from a mysterious lung disease. No treatments were available for her, and I doubt if that situation has improved. Eventually she moved into our house in Ramsey, and spent the remaining months of her life with us. Marilyn and Jack passed away far too early. They should have had the opportunity to be with, and to keep enjoying their family, and many close friends.

At Marilyn Foley's funeral mass, Neil O'Connell in the eulogy said, "We refer to those who are loving and caring as having good hearts. A good heart is the mark of a charitable and compassionate person. If I were asked whose good heart I want? I want the heart of Marilyn Foley."

The following are excerpts of letters written by Frank Murphy during his time in the U.S. Army in 1918 in France during World War I. His descriptions of war are graphic and remarkable, and allow the reader to absorb the danger of the time and the fortitude of the American soldiers. He was 27 years old, and his writing was brilliant and innocent.

Frank P. Murphy Co. A. 9th M. G. BA.E. F. Army of Occupation

I left Fort Slocum Dec. 9, 1918 arriving at Camp Greene, Charlotte, NC. Got a noisy send-off along the route. Was put in D. Co. 38th Inf.

After two months was shifted to A. Co. 9th M.G. Battalion. Did not do much but clean up the camp as

Faces from a Good Life

the weather was bad and was glad when embarkation orders came.

Left for Camp Merritt N.J. March 26th arriving on the 28th. Boarded the H.M.S. Aquitania, one of the largest and finest ships afloat on my Birthday April 1st. and pulled out the next day and slipped quietly down the bay. Spent a gloomy Easter Sunday at camp Merritt and missed the customary Easter eggs. Wrote a letter home soon after getting in to camp but could not say when we expected to go. My letter was held up for some reason until it was too late.

Between Liverpool and Southampton, we were greeted by some English nurses. We were the first Yankee soldiers they ever saw. They thought we were the real thing. After unloading our junk from the train, we hiked through the city. It is 3 miles to the English rest camp and it sure looked good to us. The scenery was (great) fine about the camp, and we liked to roam about, the weather being fine. We slept in tents about three times as big as our squad tents and oblong shaped. Here some of the boys got acquainted with that wild animal known to all soldiers as the "cootie." They were brought back from the lines by returned "Tummies."

This is where we saw the first batch of German prisoners. They were well fed and taken care of. There were twenty of us in one tent. The day we were scheduled to leave for France one of the bunch got scarlet fever so the 20 of us were quarantined, 4 sergeants 1 corporal, and 14 privates. The sick man was sent to a hospital. We stayed here two weeks— enjoying ourselves as best we could.

When we were ready to leave camp, they tried to

transfer us into the 162nd Inf. Oregon Nat. Guard, then doing M.R duty in London, Liverpool, and Southampton. Our gang didn't want it and our captain put the rollers to it. Left Southampton about the 25th of April on a cattle boat to cross the channel. There was a battalion of Australians on the scow, also a few "Tummies" just off leave to "Blighty" (sp). I talked with some of this bunch. They all agreed the "gray backs" could not be stopped. They almost had us believing it. The trip across the channel is scarier now.

On May 30th, Decoration Day, we hiked to La Trecy to entrain for the Front. Were just full of pep. 42 of us piled into a boxcar that read 40 hommes or 8 cheviot (40 Men or 8 horses). Unloaded at Mountmorail June 1st. There we got our first glimpse of the rough stuff of war. There were "tea coup" (sp) French and English and a few American wounded, lying in the depot and warehouse and along the station platform. Ambulances were rushed in, unloaded and rushed out again, Nurses and doctors working fast and hard. There were thousands of refugees going to the interior, by train, on foot and in all kinds of vehicles. The women and kids crying, but the men look grim and full of fight. The French spirit cannot be broken. It was about 6 o'clock in the evening we started hiking from Mountrail but only went about 5 miles when we loaded our trucks and struck Chezy at 12 at night and slept until 3 A.M. Got orders to lighten our packs. Got rid of all our surplus clothing and supplies. Most of the boys put their mess kits in their raincoat pockets, and left packs behind. They expected 1 or 2 days of good battle and then somebody else would have to "carry on". Before we had left the town the French soldiers had gathered up our stuff. There was a Foreign Legion Lieutenant attached to our Battalion who acted as our guide.

It was tough hiking over the hills to Chateau Thierry. The French had their artillery set up in the open fields. They didn't seem to mind being shelled. While going along we saw an antiaircraft gun in action. The Germans got a line on us coming up and shelled the road. The 7th M.G, Motorized (sp) had been rushed up and were holding Chateau Thierry.

We took a position in support on a hillside about a half kilo to the left and rear. Early the next morning the French and Americans put over a barrage. The same afternoon the French artillery blew up two bridges-.one to the left front of us about 1,500 yards. The other to the right front about 1,800 yards. This bridge was our reference object and was covered by most of our company guns.

The night of the 3rd we relieved the 7th M.G. Battalion… About 20 minutes after we were in position, the French dynamited the main bridges. There have been quite a few arguments as to who blew up their bridge. Some say the Marines did it. There was a French division between the 2nd and 3rd U.S. The 3rd held Chateau Thierry and gradually took over line from there to Moulin's. (sp). Here the French took the line to Rheine's (sp). We got a heavy shelling going into position, but had them buffaloed. We crossed the R.R. Bridge that was covered by M.G. fire and never hurt a man. Airplanes dropped flares and had us spotted. We took positions in buildings of all kinds, hotels, warehouses, round houses and the

R. R. station. Our gun position was in the Chateau Bell Vie in the south end of the city. Had our gun positioned on an upturned bureau in a bedroom facing the river. The gun was made steady by weighing it down with sand bags. To prevent the flame from our gun being spotted we hung a silk comforter up to the window and fired through it. It was necessary to keep it wet to prevent it catching fire. We held this position for 4 days, covering all roads and places of travel on the other side of the river. It was not necessary to fire after daylight as there wasn't much movement of troops. When we opened fire, they would come back strong with artillery but could not locate us. Removed to position about 200 yards in rear and on edge of woods and dug emplacement protected by railroad ties carried about ½ mile. Hard work. We hated to leave this place on account of the good chow we were able to get. The second day in town we discovered a warehouse that the Boche were unable to get at. There was enough chow to feed the Battalion for 6 months. We salvaged eggs, peas, jam, boiled ham, cocoa, canned milk, sugar, and all kinds of fancy crackers. Some front line chow for doughboys. While making trips to the warehouse we were shelled and sniped as we could easily be seen, but it was worth it.

Every cellar had its share of champagne, wine, and mineral water. We made the rounds of all the cellars and sampled the liquors. At one saloon opposite the R.R. Station my pals and I stuck our foot up on the nickel bar rail just like we would if we were home and had an old time drink with a French soldier acting as bartender. The bartender drank too,

Faces from a Good Life

then we left the place to the German Shells. There were many queer things happening around. Just back of the buildings facing the Germans, the French and American soldiers sat at tables in the yards drinking wine and singing songs.

Occasionally a Boche shell would disturb them but they carried on and made the best of it.

The town was badly shot up when we looked it over. The clock in the square was punctured by shrapnel holes. "There is a story connected with the clock I had many fine souvenirs from Chateau Thierry as the people left hurriedly and left everything behind. The Food was still on the tables as they left it. Some hospital man took over my souvenirs when I went under the dope. The 7th M.G. (Bit) relieved us after 7 days on the line. We pulled back to Viffort about 9 kilos from Chateau Thierry for 8 days rest. Here we did aircraft guard. We witnessed many air battles and fired at the Boche planes when they came within range. Took up reserve position for 2 days back of Thierry and then front line for 6 days relieving {C. LEO} of the 9th M.G. B'tlln. The shelling was heavy at daylight, but through the day we matched airplane fights. There was one scrap in which 28 machines engaged.2 of them were brought down, has odd M.G. position here, 2 men stayed with gun from 3 a.m. to 9 p.m. while the rest of squad stayed in foxholes about 30 yards to the rear.

The man at the gun just laid there in cramped position ate hard-tack and canned monkey and swore until relieved after dark. The Boche always shelled our chow "details" as they passed through the quarry back of the town. Relieved by 4th Inf. M.G. Co. while dragging our gun carts out of Thierry and passing an open space in the woods, a light was dropped by a Boche plane. We knew we were spotted. Sgt. told us all to hunt cover as he knew what was coming. Waited about 5 minutes. They shelled the road heavily for about 20 minutes to within 30 feet of where we stopped. The only available cover was an ambulance and the gun carts. Turned off main road to right into support position. About 1/4 mile back of Thierry. Just as we entered woods a big shell made a direct hit on one of our gun carts. Stayed here for 3 days.

Italian soldiers unfit for other military duty were digging trenches. Many of them were veterans of many battles. One fellow showed scars of 35M.G. wounds. We moved into position under the R.R. Bridge just east of Mezy, about 300 yards off the Marne River.

The stream running under the R.R. Bridge is called the Summerlyn River.

We relieved a French M.G. unit. Spent the 4th of July here. The night before we wondered how the boys would celebrate, but it was safe and sane in our sector except at night when Jerry slid over some gas shells and gave us the bother of wearing our masks for about 2 hours. Between the 4th and 14th of July it was very quiet in our sector but the guns on our left roared occasionally. Our artillery put over a few before they got a line on us.

They had some powerful red lights that showed up the country around like the sun in the morning. This would last about 5 minutes then all darkness again. Our signals went up for a barrage. We cut loose. The signal went up the second time. We cut loose again. After this our signal system was busted. Waited a while longer then fired on the river at different intervals. The shells came from all sides. Destructive Shells for the buildings, shrapnel dried gas for the roads and fields. I thought the bottom dropped out of hell. They had a line on everything on our side. One of the first shells wrecked our kitchen. They covered every inch of ground.

This was the worst barrage the Boche ever put over. That was the opinion of old French veterans that had been in all the big battles. It was exceptionally heavy at Crezaney and other town's further back.

Our relief was on the way up that night but was so badly shot up it never got to us. The barrage lifted on the river about 4 a.m. on the 15th but held to us until about 7: a.m. We could not occupy the field positions on account of the Boche planes just above us. The Boche Planes were strong here but the Allies planes had the air at Chateau Thierry. We set our gun up in the building over the **(P.) (Co.)** We could not distinguish between our own men and the enemy on account of the shell smoke.

We were safe from observation here and waited for a shot at the Boche. We got sight of some of them about 8:00 a.m. but they were prisoners. About 9:00 a.m. we spotted troops coming up the R.R. tracks from the wheat fields. Judging from the odd formation we knew they were the enemy. We fired on them and soon had them ducking for cover.

The battle along the river kept up all day a regular old fashioned scrap. About 7:00 p.m. things got quiet. They had advanced through the woods on our right. The drawing back of troops on our flanks endangered our men. About 11:00 p.m. we were withdrawn without waiting for relief as ordered. We were all in after a sleepless night and nothing to eat all day.

We hiked back to crossroads at **Cobrieu** with guns and equipment, and slept in reserve trenches until morning when the Boche shelled us from one place to another. The Boche entered Crezaney on the 17th, but didn't hold it long. Our artillery put up a great scrap although handicapped by not having enough men to keep the guns going.

Everybody was exhausted from the strain of the long grind. The mental strain was awful. We got what rest we could around Coburn. It was sure exciting around here. French troops coming, wounded and battle-weary men being rushed to the rear.

There were some airplane battles. The Boche planes flying low and machine gunning our camp. They had easy targets to shoot at us along the roads but did little damage. We were in the woods about 200 yards from Cobrieu when General Pershing was there looking things over. He ordered the town cleared as it was a mess of wreckage after the 18th. This was a prize rest place as it was safe.

CHAPTER 10

Notes of a Frustrated American

I HAVE BEEN a member of the, Freedom From Religion (FFR) movement for many years, and would have been an active member, but the situation did not present itself. Most cases of religious encroachment on government and schools are conducted in the southern states, and the upper mid-west. Thankfully, I have always resided in New York or New Jersey where people have enough sense to limit their religious practices to their homes, and places of worship. That term, *worship,* startles me. Whenever I hear it used in the present. Worship, sounds to me as if one is speaking about terrible Mayan or Aztec religious ceremonies that usually culminated with human sacrifice, but I find it demeaning to modern people who otherwise believe in science and logic. I actually don't care what it is anyone believes, as long as they keep it to themselves, their family and good friends, and do not annoy others with their religious beliefs. However, I would like to see everyone claiming religious membership especially the clergy, to practice the tenets of their religion, which usually include, good and fair treatment of others, ethical, moral and charitable life styles, and especially, concern, and help for the poor and sick. However, we are daily witnessing the god-fearing ultra-religious Republicans in Washington, and in many state legislatures do everything possible to limit voting by African Americans. Their total lack of humanity now makes it illegal in places to provide water to anyone waiting in line to vote especially in warm places like Georgia. This reminds me of the reports of Jews in the 1940s packed into railroad box cars on their way to Auschwitz, and certain death, begging for water, which was sold to them by Eastern European railroad workers, who demanded cash, jewelry or time pieces for a half cup of water.

My philosophy therefore is to leave the rest of us alone, and you may practice your ceremonies, as much as you like. I knew a married couple who had a home down the road from our vacation lake house in Pennsylvania. Both were educated, and had satisfying jobs, and two great children. However, whenever I was with the male of the couple he would say to me, "Cynthia and I have made a personal decision for Christ." Not sure of what he meant the first time, I nodded to be polite. He later explained that he was an evangelical committed to bringing "The Good News" to "heathens," (my word) like me. After hearing several more times about their being "born again" and their decision for Christ, I knew that this individual, whom I had considered a friend, was attempting to recruit me to accept his religious beliefs. I was insulted, and no longer cared to associate with someone who didn't respect my lack of faith, which I didn't discuss, and hadn't any effect on him.

All super religious activities are, in my opinion, detrimental to democracy. The Evangelicals are the most threatening due to their large numbers, and are followed by the Satmar Hasidic cult, a law and norm avoiding community, that's growing geometrically in which, women are treated as breeders, and children receive inadequate education in order that they remain ignorant of American culture. The Satmar are overwhelmingly far rightists, and Trump supporters, and their communities are operated as authoritarian places. They have established something of the ghetto, that their European forbearers were kept in, because they were Jewish. All of the ultra-religious groups constantly work to flout the separation of state and religion, as put forth in the First Amendment. Sadly, they often are successful.

I'm an out and proud liberal Democrat, like my parents and grandparents. Democrats are smarter than Republicans. We care about others. I'm referring of course only to the Democrats, in office after the racist plan known as the Southern Strategy was accomplished. In 1968, Barry Goldwater the Republican candidate, while running for president openly appealed to the inherent racism of southern white voters. Richard Nixon continued the Southern Strategy rather successfully. Longtime southern Democrats who loved the Jim Crow laws that fully controlled the activities of African Americans, in the states known as the Old South, registered as Republicans, and voted for Nixon. Trump, of course proved my point about Republicans being stupid by their accepting, and then completely supporting, the most corrupt, inept, and embarrassing administration in our nation's history.

The Evangelical movement involves millions of American Protestants, and some Catholics who believe the Bible is all true and without error, and that one must accept Jesus Christ, in order to be "saved." Going along with that I assume morality, charity, honesty and fair treatment of everyone are also important attributes for these good evangelicals. However, early on in his campaign, Trump, who had none of these good qualities was able to capture the backing of the evangelical leadership, and their obedient flocks. Almost immediately Jerry Falwell, Jr. then president of the evangelical Liberty University publicly and with great fanfare backed Trump's candidacy for president. Other evangelical leaders quickly fell in line because they were promised cash, and an end to Roe v. Wade by a thrice married man, still having sexual relations with prostitutes, and admitting to sexual assault of women in general. Trump is also a racist, unscrupulous in business, never having given one dollar to a charitable cause, and accepting and complimenting, the violent extremists showing up at his circus like rallies. A perfect person for young evangelicals to emulate. Jerry Falwell, Jr., eventually crashed and became irrelevant when photos of him and his wife having a threesome with the pool boy, in a Florida motel they owned were made public.

Liberty University, has not been the same since Jerry Jr. resigned as its president. It has become a punch line for late night television, and is mired in law suits. It's believed, by credible people that Trump's lawyer and fixer, was somehow able to acquire the Falwell family photos, and blackmailed Jerry junior into supporting Trump early in the campaign. Recently, I have received many email solicitations from Liberty University's online degree program that ranges from undergraduate degrees to the Ph.D. In the space asking for my area of interest I entered, "I want the, Family Values Seminar, taught by Jerry Falwell, Jr." Strangely I haven't heard from Liberty lately.

On January 6, 2021, a day that truly will live in infamy, along with the 9/11 tragedy and Pearl Harbor, Trump, actually attempted a coup d'état, an illegal seizure of power, the overthrow of our government when he lost the election to Joseph Biden. The evidence that the election was honest and legal in every sense is over whelming, but the

Republicans, support everything and anything that Trump says and does no matter how illegal, absurd or stupid is his behavior. Only two national Republicans, Liz Chaney and Adam Kinzinger are honest and worried about the nation's shift toward totalitarianism, and the Republican Party's abandonment of our Constitution. Actually, the Republicans have lost their party, and gained everything they want.

Democrats are often accused of being disorganized and unable to agree on anything. It's true, but that's why we are better than Republicans. We care about so many different issues so we sometimes lose track of the main issue of the day. We want to include and help everyone. We are the real Americans, diverse, caring, honest and passionate about our causes, and our democracy. Republicans on the other hand want only power, and don't break ranks for any reason. They don't want African Americans, voting, they are opposed to immigration, and shudder at the "Browning" of America. They actually believe that a white Christian nation will be achieved, and that the Jews, Blacks, Hispanics and Muslims will disappear. They follow what their leaders dictate with the threat of personal and professional destruction hanging over them, if they stray.

The rank and file Republicans, are ready and willing to do violence to anyone who their Nazi type leaders say is the enemy of their getting what they want. Republicans who lose elections insist they were cheated. They actually believe they were illegally defeated by corrupt election officials, voting machines that didn't count votes for them, and unregistered voters, brought in by the thousands, to vote for the opposition candidate. Republicans spend millions in court fights that actually prove there was no election fraud, but that doesn't stop them. If they lose they believe they were robbed and may physically attack the winning candidate. There is no limit to their madness, which we are witnessing daily in Arizona. The Republican candidates, for state and national offices there are anti-democracy, anti-actual elections, and terrified of the rising number of voters with Hispanic backgrounds who have lived in Arizona much longer than any of the Republicans including their last candidate for governor who is originally from Illinois.

Donald Trump who reads on the fourth-grade level didn't read Hitler's Mein Kampf (My Struggle), but people around him did, and are following the monster's playbook. Even more obvious is the Republican's faithfully following Joseph Goebbels' propaganda blueprint for the taking over a nation. Goebbels was Hitler's closest friend, advisor and acolyte. His careful plan of lying to the Germans regularly, constantly and masterfully, brought Hitler to power and maintained him until he had control of life and death of all Germans, and then most Europeans. *(Goebbels' plan has been reproduced in exact detail at the book's end.)*

Whom do I blame for the course of events that have divided our nation, not just recently, but always? I blame Abraham Lincoln, yes, Lincoln, one of the most revered presidents because he saved the Union. Yes the nation stayed together, but racism was forever institutionalized. Lincoln was ambivalent regarding slavery, and possibly would have compromised with Southern leaders by ignoring their desertion, and allowing them to return to the Union as they realized the South could not sustain itself economically. Instead, he waged an all-out war against the South, in order to save it as a part of the United States. Southern society was based on the English aristocracy system, enjoyed there for centuries, with a distain of human rights, and dignity that continues, to the present time. **(Read New York Times article, "The Brutal System That Still Rules Alabama's Black Belt, Sunday July 31, 2022)** Growing cotton was economically profitable only because slaves were the workers picking it during inhuman conditions. Perhaps if Lincoln did not demand that the Union, which was only eighty-five years old at the time remain intact, the South may have eventually petitioned to return without slavery as it had become unprofitable, and had ended throughout the British Empire in 1834. There may have been a peaceful settlement instead of the most destructive war in our nation's history.

Perhaps then Booth would not have murdered Abraham Lincoln, and Andrew Johnson the most terrible destructive president until Donald Trump would not have ascended to the presidency. Johnson a southerner encouraged the institution of Black Codes throughout the South to control the former slaves, practically returning them to slavery for another century. Because when they were freed they began to organize to gain political power, and several from the south were actually elected to Congress, and to state legislatures.

The Military Reconstruction Act passed by Congress after the Civil War ended was the greatest social program, and best public policy project ever undertaken by the government of the United States during the nation's entire history. However, President Andrew Johnson made sure Reconstruction, which was designed to bring all former slaves into American society was a failure. Instead Black people in the South, were again held back from achieving through the institutionalization of legally enforced segregation, in schools, housing, restaurants, retail stores, churches, theaters, and public restrooms. Lynching became ordinary, and sometimes carried out with the approval of sheriffs and police chiefs. Only certain jobs and careers were open to the former slaves, and they were made to work as sharecroppers, without being paid a single penny, in order to survive and not go hungry sometimes on the same land they worked while enslaved.

President Woodrow Wilson, instituted the "One drop rule" that forbade anyone with one drop of "Negro blood" from gaining employment by the U.S. Government over a certain basic job level. In fact, those identified as "Colored" in the Wilson administration working over the basic level were demoted or fired. The "One drop rule" was adopted by eighteen states, and was the law until struck down by the United Sates Supreme Court in 1967.

Black persons, didn't always fare much better in northern states as the tradition of segregation was also there, but was more subtle. Even after landmark legislation was passed by Congress in the 1960s, and Browne v. Board of Education ended legal school segregation, negative attitudes toward Black Americans, by so many white Americans, remained cast in concrete. I believe that is the real legacy of Abraham Lincoln and that he realized at some point, he had allowed a terrible crisis to unfold. However, Lincoln, accepted no criticism of his war. He jailed newspaper reporters, editors, publishers and others, without the benefit of Habeas Corpus who were publicly against the war between the states. He had an anti-war congressman hunted down and chased to Canada to escape arrest. Lincoln was brilliant, but stubborn and not likely to admit to a gigantic error, the war that had the effect of permanently enforcing the nation's sectionalism.(8)

As a result of the terribly divisive Civil War, begun by southerners who chose blood and death over political compromise, and northern generals, who burned and destroyed southern cities, as if everyone living there was their enemy the suspicions and hatred by southerners still exists.

Indiana, Home of the Ku Klux Klan

Today there are Republican Party candidates openly calling for a white Christian America, as if they are residing in the State of Indiana during the 1920s.

After the Civil War ended scores of southern plantation owners made their way north and settled in Indiana. The attitudes of the planters didn't change over time, and by 1920 Indiana was controlled by the Ku Klux Klan supported by the state's Republican Party. Indiana's governor, its legislators, mayors, police chiefs, ministers were members of the Klan, as were 40% of Indiana's residents, and at the time, the Klan's enemies were the Catholic immigrants arriving from Europe. Black people, and Jews were not yet numerous enough in Indiana to warrant the Klan's attention.

The Klan, and Indiana's Republicans were motivated by the "100% American" phrase which meant, 100% white, Protestant, English speaking, and native born are the real Americans who follow the American flag and the cross. It is believed that Sinclair Lewis said it first, "When fascism comes to America, it will be led by a cross, wrapped in the flag." The Indiana Klan stayed in power until its bombastic, immoral, degenerate leader, D.C. Stephenson, raped and murdered a young woman.

Will murder, he was accused of rape, be the final straw to break the back politically and actually of, Donald J. Trump? Trump has committed federal and state crimes so numerous that, Capone and Gotti, would be envious. He possesses similar charisma as the late, D.C. Stephenson, and other tyrants and dictators namely, Mussolini, Franco, Stalin and Hitler. Trump, actually sees himself, and his corrupt rancid family as the future of America forever. Make no mistake, Trump isn't the average racist scammer. He was raised to be dishonest, and taught by the worst people possible to believe in no one, but himself, to avoid charity, good deeds, and paying debts. He has gotten away with every bit of terrible behavior that he is proud of, and denies his disgusting actions, because those around him pretend he's a normal person. Looking in a mirror, Trump only sees what's right for himself. No one, not his children, or dead American soldiers, he called them "suckers" for serving, and dying for their country, have an effect on his self-serving colossal ego. As president, he actually refused to visit an American Military cemetery while in France because it was raining. As proof of Trump's invulnerability, the Republican Party at its annual meeting declared the January 6 insurrection "Legitimate Political Discourse." However, Special Prosecutor, Jack Smith has indicted Trump for crimes against the United States. Atlanta District Attorney, Fani Willis has also indicted Trump on numerous felony charges against the State of Georgia. Trump's New York real estate portfolio has been successfully assailed by New York's Attorney General Trish James. The Trump family potentially will loose control of all of their buildings, and be forbidden to do business in New York. It took decades to weed out the Klan from control in Indiana, and it has been a decade since Trump became a threat to the Constitution, our legal system and our way of life.

The Texas legislature, led by the hollow criminal Governor Greg Abbot, declared recently that Joseph R. Biden, had not been elected President of the United States in 2020. That I believe is a declaration of independence for Texas, which should break away from the rest of the United States, and reinstate the Lone Star Republic so the state may continue to make its own rules and defy established norms. However, the vast amount of federal funds received annually by Texas will immediately dry up, which will make the state's felonious negligence regarding electrical service, education, health care, and voting rights even more destructive to working class Texans.

Insurrection, which to the understanding of most intelligent people is a high crime. It is treason and in this case, the attempted overthrow of our government. That basic concept is taught, perhaps not in Texas, in high school history classes as the worst crime against the government of the United States. The January 6 insurrection was planned, carried out and defended by the treasonous, degenerate, disgraced president Donald J. Trump. He was twice impeached by the House of Representatives. As predicted Republican senators did not believe that treason, and carrying out an insurrection was a high enough crime to convict the invulnerable, Trump. Watch out Americans, totalitarianism is on its way, and yes it can happen here. The January 6 Hearings, by the House of Representatives, have proven that Trump had knowingly and willingly planned to over throw the presidential election, and remain in power. For the first time in our history, which used to allow us to reassure the world there is always a peaceful transfer of power, a defeated president attempted to be king.

(8) *The Real Lincoln,* Thomas J. Dilorenzo, Crown Forum.
It wasn't About Slavery: The Great Lie of the Civil War, Samuel W. Mitcham, Blackstone Publishing.

The Social Compact

Since the time I was a young man, I have had the desire to somehow assist people who were not able to help themselves, and didn't receive the care they needed, in order to sustain a healthy and stable life. I was influenced by an early television series titled "Eastside, Westside," starring George C. Scott, as a cardigan sweater wearing social worker, in an urban setting. I found my way to the social welfare and education fields first by working as an administrator and later counselor/case worker in the Anti-Poverty Program initiated by John F. Kennedy, after being influenced, it was said, by Michael Harrington's seminal book *The Other America*. The influential national effort was instituted by Lyndon Johnson. Looking back prior to the program's beginning in the 1960s, clearly welfare assistance was punitive, and contributed to the dissolution of families, and destroyed ambitions, and hope for advancement.

The inhumanity continues, fueled by Republican's appeal to white evangelicals, who have been socialized to oppose abortion. Most Republican legislators, on either state or federal level, are men who really could not care less about the "rights" of unborn children, since they don't care about the rights of existing children. They prove that by fighting any assistance to single mothers, subsidies for child care, better health plans that are free or affordable, food stamp expansion and subsidies for decent housing for families with young children. A recent *New York Times* article quoted Gloria Steinem who said in the 1970s, "If men could get pregnant, abortion would be a sacrament, but they can't and it isn't." However, the Republican Party needed something to rally around that didn't cost anything. Abortion was the answer, and Republicans are using it as their reason for being in power, and striving to rule the nation. Even rape, and incest that cause pregnancies are not immune from the highly restrictive anti-abortion laws that were introduced by the male legislators, in at least three dozen states. In the State of Louisiana, the legislature has introduced a bill that would charge women who had an abortion, with murder. Can you guess how many white upper income women would be arrested? The answer is none.

The historic Supreme Court decision, Roe v. Wade has, been scuttled, by the Court's inhumane rightists consisting of three Trump appointees and two holdovers. One holdover, is a moron, who has not written an opinion since being appointed to the court, decades ago, and whose wife is a paid operative for extreme ultra conservative groups, heavily financed by some of America's richest casually fascist families. He has openly and blatantly accepted graft in the form of cash, property, travel, and luxurious gifts including a $260,000 motor home. The other is a mean, mentally defective individual. True to their obstructive behavior, Republicans, fought the appointment, by President Biden, of an African American woman to the court. They practically are screaming that the appointment of such a person must be prohibited, since it's unfair and prejudicial and horrors "Affirmative Action." Senator Blackburn of Tennessee complained that an appointee to the Supreme Court should not be announced while Russia was invading Ukraine. She really meant, a Black woman should not be nominated at all. Personally, I would like to see nine Black women on the Court. However, Trump, and Mitch McConnell, appointed, Amy Comey Barrett, a lawyer who has never taken a deposition, never has done any public service, and had only three years as a judge, on the circuit court of appeals. She taught, in a mid-western law school for a while, and was appointed to the court before Justice Ginsberg's funeral had even been planned. Her appointment was engineered by the demon fascist Mitch McConnell who is successfully destroying the democratic process in America, in favor of a one-party totalitarian system financed by hundreds of million dollars contributed by secretive American fascists.

Republicans, somehow believe ending abortion is the way to secure votes from young white women, and women living in upper middle-class suburbs, who look down on African Americans and Hispanics. I imagine that may work in places like Mississippi and West Virginia our two poorest states, but hopefully nowhere else. On the heels of ending

Roe v. Wade, the Nazi inspired Justices on the Supreme Court declared that everyone can have a gun everywhere in the United States, and the states had no right to limit the public carrying of deadly weapons. Soon passengers on airplanes will have the right to carry guns, as will anyone anywhere else. Let's arm everyone at every age, so that if someone annoys you it's all right to shoot him, as they have allowed in Wisconsin with the Kyle Rittenhouse not guilty decision, freeing an admitted murderer who cried at his trial.

The next project for Republicans, will probably involve identifying and burning witches, since they want to turn back the clock, and stop progress on all social issues, the environment and public education, I nominate, Marjory Taylor Green as their first witch to be burned, since she hears QAnon messages, and has created unbelievable havoc, while pretending to be a member of Congress. At President Biden's first State of the Union, Greene heckled the president throughout his speech, even during the moment when he sadly mentioned his deceased son, who had served in Afghanistan. Have you no decency Marjory? No, you are disgusting, a rodent, and a person without any moral compass, without any reason to be alive. Marjory's latest insult to Americans and the Constitution is her describing herself as, "a Christian Nationalist," in a similar manner as the idiot who was the last Republican nominee for the governorship of Pennsylvania. He has actually advocated the death penalty for any woman under going an abortion. They ignore the separation of church and state clause of the Constitution, but incorrectly worship the Second Amendment, which clearly states, citizens may be armed as members of "A well regulated militia." That phrase was included, in order to be prepared for a possible British invasion, as an aftermath of the, American Revolution, which did occur in 1812.

The Republican Party, following its maximum leader, the disgraced degenerate Donald J. Trump is a collection of the nastiest group of people ever assembled in this country. The, Bund, meetings of the 1930s held in arenas as large as Madison Square Garden were anti-American in purpose similar to present day Republican assemblies. Bund members were sad unimportant people. Main stream Republicans are not. They meet online not only in arenas, and attack our government, and President Biden for his dealing effectively with Russian aggression in Ukraine. Russia's attack on a peaceful nation has spiraled out of control for dictator Putin, recently called "A genius" by Trump.

The European Union, and Britain, and the rest of the free world are solidly in step with us. Russia, must be stopped before it decides to try to annex Europe, and a world war erupts again. Republicans are praising Putin, and condemning Joe Biden with the full force of their media outlets especially Fox that caters to weak minded Americans. Recently fired from Fox, the treasonous anti-American Tucker Carlson a Trump servant much like Goebbels was to Hitler has millions of working-class viewers believing that even union members, should be against unions, that Obama Care is un-American, and Social Security and Medicare, are evidence of Socialism in America even though the Social Security Act was passed in 1935, and is the only source of retirement income for millions of American families. Robert Reich, has publicly and repeatedly called Carlson, "The most dangerous demagogue since Trump, and one of the worst Americans." It's impossible to convince the feeble minded, in the Fox TV audience that they are rallying and voting against their own interests, and that's what dictators count on.

These same individuals have been convinced that inflation is their greatest enemy and it's Joe Biden's fault that prices of some consumer items and gasoline are higher than last year. The oil companies will earn billions due to the chaos caused by Putin's war. The American government does not in any manner control oil production, which was lower than usual for the last two years due to Covid's influence that reduced gasoline use for travel, and the increased availability of electric powered automobiles.

Of course President Biden, inherited the Covid pandemic that was largely ignored by the galactically stupid Trump who ignores anything that does not serve his immediate and slimy personal agenda. While effectively dealing with Covid, President Biden's policies have also reduced unemployment to an historic low, boosted the economy to an historic high level, and encouraged salaries of hourly workers to be raised to a livable level, and passing the infrastructure bill, which will benefit everyone. And remember Trump did not allow any of Joe Biden's transition team even to speak with anyone, in the administration until after President Biden was inaugurated. An unheard of waste of almost three months of learning, that was destroyed by Trump. Meanwhile, Republicans have fought every piece of legislation, especially for voting rights and family assistance, aided by two Democrats, who are obviously in the pay of right-wing elements, devoted to keeping working class Americans from progressing. However, President Joseph Biden was successful in getting passed by Congress the most sweeping social legislative program, since the New Deal was created by Franklin D. Roosevelt, and enacted between 1933 and 1939.

Inventing Donald J. Trump

The dirty little secret of how Donald Trump became the Republican candidate for President of the United States was revealed in an article, in the *New York Times Magazine*. The long, well written, comprehensive explanation, authored by Elizabeth Zerofsky outlines in detail the creation of Trump's candidacy by an ultra-conservative "think tank," in California called the Claremont Institute. The people at Claremont, are the spawn of the ridiculous and pretentious William F. Buckley, the father of America's casual fascism.

The Claremont Institute is a forty-year collection of angry, self-appointed, pseudo intellectuals who write and publish their own journals, newsletters, books and on-line articles that whine about, "Joe Biden's embrace of the left-wing part of the Democratic Party's moral critique of America." In other words they argue, Americans who believe that America is a racist county are "non-Americans." In simpler terms, away from the imagined highbrow philosophical justifications put out by the Claremont bunch, they are white supremacists of the worst order.

The Claremont boys, no women seem to be involved, with the exception of certifiably crazy Marjorie Taylor Green, who shows up at some Claremont functions, actually claim to believe that racism has never existed in the United States. Further they claim that the government's desire to democratize our society is unconstitutional, and that our system of education has regularly lied about the contributions of Black, and Brown, and Indigenous people to the development and progress of the nation as they claim, there haven't been any contributions from these people that have made a difference according to Claremont's self-identified geniuses.

The *Times Magazine* article asserts that Claremont Institute Senior Fellow Michael Anton turned Trump into a legitimate candidate of necessary change, **"The initial assumption was, this guy is a buffoon, a reality TV star, not even an amateur politician, not a politician** at all, there's nothing serious about any of his ideas, or any of his programs, therefore no serious person could possibly support him or make an argument on his behalf. And then we did it." Claremont Institute Board Chairman Thomas Klingenstein said, "If here is within the conservative movement a kind of intellectual justification for Trump, it came from Claremont."

Claremont Institute appears at present to be solely financed by the secretive New York financial fund manager Thomas Klingenstein. He's a partner in the advisory firm Cohen, Klingenstein and Marks, which does not have a web site, and provides only the public information required to maintain its license in New York State. There is even less information regarding Thomas Klingenstein publicly available. I found a video presentation on line, in which Klingenstein gives a formal speech at a podium, in front of an audience of indeterminable size. He claims, "Trump was born for the current crisis, and must be supported by conservatives, and re-elected." Klingenstein, insists there is, "a cold war against wouk communism." He also espouses that the American government is "a totalitarian regime, making all identity groups equal with a goal to end America." "Trump," he says," awakened the public to that fact." A "strongman" (dictator) is needed to control the forces of equality for all, says, Thomas Klingenstein, He has brought the desire of many, for an authoritarian, fascist, white government out from under the rock where it lay with the worms and insects intertwined with our history, and now is promoted by the neo-Nazis at Claremont.

Claremont Institute, in its office park setting east of Los Angeles has been the intellectual home of many American Fascists including John Eastman, who convinced the weak-minded Trump that poor, dumb Mike Pence didn't have to count the electoral votes making Joe Biden, president. Eastman has been indicted in Georgia for election tampering, and faces years in prison if convicted. He is also, at this time, an unindicted co-conspirator in the federal case against Trump in Washington, DC. It appears likely that Eastman will spend his last years in one or another prison.

Mike Pompeo former Secretary of State under Trump who also had a problem with democracy, and in his mind is a future presidential candidate, was recently honored, by the Claremont Institute. The disgusting Ron DeSantis the governor of Florida, also in the race for the 2024 Republican presidential nomination, is a Claremont regular. He is actually infusing the Institute's poisonous view of United States history into Florida's fragile public education system, and the few views held by Clarence Thomas, were shaped by the Claremont Institute.

Woodrow Wilson, the twenty-eighth President of the United States, is a patron saint of the Claremont Institute. Wilson's view of the Declaration of Independence and Constitution were, "antithetical to human freedom, therefore, have no teaching concerning the best regime or even ranking legitimate regimes," and is accepted as Claremont's reason for being. Wilson, a noted racist, and creator of the, "one drop rule" that excluded Black Americans from government jobs, provided the "new view of the nature of man," followed closely by the Claremont Institute, in all of its policies and publications.

Klingenstein, the Board Chairman, appears to be most concerned with preventing the teaching of "critical race theory," which has become an excuse for the right wingers to interfere in the teaching of American history. They cannot define the term. Claremont's "scholars" have repeatedly insisted that the nation's public universities, which are tax supported, be defunded as the history classes offered on hundreds of college campuses, "teach young people to despise their country." Apparently, the truth has no place at the Claremont Institute. Institute.

It's henchmen, convinced the legislature of the State of Idaho to cut $2.5 million from social-justice programs that "penetrated" Idaho's universities. Also, college students in Idaho, have been banned from affirming tenets associated with critical race theory, a clear violation of the First Amendment. Can we look forward to book burnings in Idaho and curricula approved by Republican politicians with connections to the Claremont Institute?

And on the seventh day, Clermont created, Trump. The acceptance of a "Buffoon" by the self-appointed arbiters of American politics and values provided the blessing required by conservative Republicans who had captured their party's essence. Claremont alums flooded the Trump administration as appointees to federal agencies, and in the White House. They accused the Democrats, of using the pandemic, which Trump, essentially ignored, "to unconstitutionally change election laws to benefit themselves." The Claremont espionage team, also proposed the breaking up of the CIA, getting rid of the Department of Education, and the Equal Employment Opportunity Commission, and stopping "Ceaseless importation of Third World foreigners with no tradition or, taste of experience in liberty."

So why Donald Trump for president? Even a casual reading of Trump's history makes it clear that he's stupid, easily flattered and manipulated, hungry for power and money, is an under educated racist, believing in his own authority as the final determination by ignoring laws and the judicial system. However, Trump was perfect for the Claremont gang who fantasized themselves as the instrument returning America to a white controlled nation. That was due to Trump's in-your-face, norm-crushing style, which they correctly predicted would appeal to under educated white males, working class Americans, and underemployed individuals such as those who wait for the coal mines to open, and the steel mills to again pollute the air over entire cities.

Elizabeth Zerofsky's article, in the August 8, 2022, *New York Times Magazine* exposed the Clermont Institute's mission, **"to shape a Trumpian vision for American conservatism that started a revolution, and is far from finished.**

⋄⇒◯⇐⋄

Goebbels' Principles, and Adolf Trump
Also known as the Republican Party's Trump Playbook

Dr. Joseph Goebbels, besides being an intriguing character, was the Propaganda Minister for Hitler's Third Reich. He was recognized as a master of propaganda as his work was studied after WWII. Goebbels did not survive to enjoy the recognition; he and his wife committed suicide on 1 May 1945, a week before the final collapse of the Third Reich.

After the war, US personnel discovered a very large diary dictated by Goebbels. In it are his principles of propaganda. Leonard Doob's 1950 article details them from a translation of the diary by Louis Lochner (1948). **(Tucker Carlson is the embodiment of Goebbels for our time)**

It is actually uncanny when Goebbel's principles are compared to Trump's ravings at his ludicrous gatherings, they are exactly the same. Trump is using all of the techniques employed by Adolf Hitler to capture the German public in the 1930s. Many of our fellow Americans whose grandfathers fought fascism have embraced Trump who obviously is a senile and dangerous individual devoted to destroying America's consistent attempt to enhance the promise of the Constitution's equal treatment for everyone.

Recently Trump's rhetoric clearly echoed German Nazis. He said, "We pledge to you that we will root out the Communists, Marxists, Racists, and Radical Left thugs that live like vermin within the confines of our country, lie, steal, and cheat on Elections, and will do anything possible, whether legally or illegally, to destroy America, and the American Dream." His speeches that echo Hitler, Mussolini and Franco almost exactly were analyzed by Dr. Heather Cox Richardson, the distinguished American historian and Professor at Boston College. Dr. Richardson is the author of the daily newsletter, "Letters from an American," which is free, and available as an email. I encourage everyone to subscribe, and read Dr. Richardson's comprehensive exposure of the sins and crimes of Trump, the MAGAs, and the Republican Party, which are presented with citations daily.

Trump has the incredible audacity to announce his program of fascist control of the United States government if he were again in power. The center of his madness is his promise to aggressively round up all undocumented persons residing in our nation, no matter how long they have been here. He would use the National Guard of states in support of his inhumanity, which will cause the sane states on the east and west coasts to use their National Guard units to repel the other soldiers. Hence, a new civil war would enfold. Trump's plan, which his pet Nazi Stephen Miller developed, calls for the establishment of concentration camps for the holding of the undocumented people. Miller has been disowned by all of his Jewish family who three generations ago escaped from Hitler's Europe, and found haven in the United States.

Not satisfied with causing a civil war, Trump also plans to destroy the Justice Department and to turn the FBI into his own agency of revenge, similar to Hitler's SS. He would eliminate the Department of Education, the EPA, the National Institutes of Health, which ends cancer research, the IRS, and any other part of the government that could threaten his plan to be president for life. He is actually running on this agenda, and Americans are not sufficiently terrified.

Hitler's Basic Principles

These principles are abstracted from Jowett & O'Donnell.

- Avoid abstract ideas - appeal to the emotions.
- Constantly repeat just a few ideas. Use stereotyped phrases.
- Give only one side of the argument.
- Continuously criticize your opponents.
- Pick out one special "enemy" for special vilification.

Goebbels' Principles of Propaganda

When reading these propaganda principles, keep in mind that they were applied in wartime (WWII) and involve issues that don't arise otherwise. It's a long list, but Goebbels was dealing with the complexity of an all-out war. While reading them you may realize that some of the principles are generally applicable and not limited to wartime. Some might be quite familiar today.

It is interesting to note that Goebbels' principles derive from Hitler's own ideas of propaganda.

1. **Propagandists must have access to intelligence concerning events and public opinion.**
2. **Propaganda must be planned and executed by only one authority.**
    1. *It must issue all the propaganda directives.*
    2. *It must explain propaganda directives to important officials and maintain their morale.*
    3. *It must oversee other agencies' activities which have propaganda consequences.*
3. **The Propaganda consequences of an action must be considered in planning that action.**
4. **Propaganda must affect the enemy's policy and actions.**
    1. *By suppressing propagandistically desirable material which can provide the enemy with useful intelligence.*
    2. *By openly disseminating propaganda whose contents or tone causes the enemy to draw the desired conclusions.*
    3. *By goading the enemy into revealing vital information about himself.*
    4. *By making no reference to a desired enemy activity when any reference would discredit that activity.*
5. **Declassified, operational information must be available to implement a propaganda campaign.**
6. **To be perceived, propaganda must evoke the interest of an audience and must be transmitted through an attention-getting medium.**
7. **Credibility alone must determine whether propaganda output should be true or false.**

8. The purpose, content, and effectiveness of enemy propaganda; the strength and effects of an expose'; and the nature of current propaganda campaigns determine whether enemy propaganda should be ignored or refuted.
9. Credibility, intelligence, and the possible effects of communicating determine whether propaganda materials should be censored.
10. Material from enemy propaganda may be utilized in operations when it helps diminish that enemy's prestige or lends support to the propagandist's own objective.
11. Black rather than white propaganda must be employed when the latter is less credible or produces undesirable effects.
12. Propaganda may be facilitated by leaders with prestige.
13. Propaganda must be carefully timed.
    1. *The communication must reach the audience ahead of competing propaganda.*
    2. *A propaganda campaign must begin at the optimum moment.*
    3. *A propaganda theme must be repeated, but not beyond some point of diminishing effectiveness.*
14. Propaganda must label events and people with distinctive phrases or slogans.
    1. *They must evoke responses which the audience previously possesses.*
    2. *They must be capable of being easily learned.*
    3. *They must be utilized again and again, but only in appropriate situations.*
    4. *They must be boomerang-proof.*
15. Propaganda to the home front must prevent the raising of false hopes which can be blasted by future events.

16. **Propaganda to the home front must create an optimum anxiety level.**
    1. *Propaganda must reinforce anxiety concerning the consequences of defeat.*
    2. *Propaganda must diminish anxiety (other than that concerning the consequences of defeat) which is too high and cannot be reduced by people themselves.*
17. **Propaganda to the home front must diminish the impact of frustration.**
    1. *Inevitable frustrations must be anticipated.*
    2. *Inevitable frustrations must be placed in perspective.*
18. **Propaganda must facilitate the displacement of aggression by specifying the targets for hatred.**
19. **Propaganda cannot immediately affect strong counter-tendencies; instead, it must offer some form of action or diversion, or both.**

These would be principles guiding the conduct of propaganda operations.

References

Goebbels' Principles of Propaganda, Leonard W. Doobs, Public Opinion Quarterly, Fall 1950 pp.419-442

Propagation and Persuasion; Jowett & O'Donnell

Thanks to Jim Richardson, who supplied this piece, and who sadly passed away July 2, 2022.

A description of the Trump adoring Republicans written over a half century ago by a historian forced from Europe to escape Hitler.

The ideal subject of totalitarian rule is not the convinced Nazi or the convinced Communist, but people for whom the distinction between fact and fiction, and the distinction between true and false no longer exist.

Hannah Arendt, The Origins of Totalitarianism (1967)

THE END
(Of this book, but I hope not the end of democracy)

Books by Ron Kase

Fiddler's Return (Includes the novels *Fiddler's Elbow and Fiddler's revenge)*. An award-winning novel that provides the possible answer to one of the 20th Century's greatest mysteries, the death of Princess Diana, which opened up an inquiry into the Royal Firm the Queen's billion dollar corporation.

A Time in Ybor City An extraordinarily beautiful mixed-race woman travels through the 1930s from Prohibition to the dawn of World War II moving from domestic servant to mistress of a wealthy industrialist, and on to a loving, but doomed, relationship with maestro George Gershwin, while he completes the operatic masterpiece "Porgy & Bess." Filled with the history of Tampa's exotic Ybor City the home of Cuban culture in America, readers are introduced to the place, and the people that produced legendary handmade clear Havana cigars for a half century.

Kavanagh's Dilemma Just like Leopold Bloom, James Joyce's protagonist, in the epic *Ulysses,* Kavanagh an American social work professor is inconveniently influenced by his relationships with women. He is a seeker of passion and intimacy, with the women he finds desirable. Kavanagh and Bloom are Irish Jews the decedents of the members of small migrations from Eastern Europe, in the late 1890s that somehow found their way to Ireland. Kavanagh's complex attempts at love involve three exceptional women, an African American TV executive, a Catholic nun, and an Irish physician.

The Murder Bureau The post-vulgar Trump presidency found the nation still facing nativist white supremacists that had banded together to continue their attack on American values. A newly elected president was heroically striving to restore the nation's position of leadership, in the world that Trump had purposely deteriorated, at the bidding of Russia's Vladimir Putin. The new president assembles a group of six people. They are granted the responsibility of arranging the permanent elimination of individuals and groups that have as their mission the end of democracy, in the United States. The newly assembled committee becomes known to its members as *The Murder Bureau.*

New Jersey's Meadowlands (with co-author Robert Ceberio). From the time the Dutch arrived in the 1600s, the Meadowlands has had a storied and mysterious history. Nearly destroyed by centuries of abuse, Meadowlands waterways are now reclaimed, as are thirty square miles of protected wetlands. "The most definitive book about the Meadowlands ever written." *Northjerseynews.com*

Bill Miller's Riviera (with co-author Tom Austin). Bill Miller's Riviera nightclub was perched on the edge of the Palisades over the Hudson River, and attracted the most sought after performers of the day. The Riviera had stunning showgirls, famous bands, and a secret gambling casino. Frank Sinatra, Sammy Davis, Jr., Ava Gardner, Sugar Ray Robinson, Micky Mantle, and the most dangerous members of the Mafia including Meyer Lansky, were regulars at Bill Miller's Riviera.

Available from Amazon, B&N.com, and all booksellers.

Author's Page

A long time ago, my then, almost middle age parents had a baby, a boy. They named him Ronald after English born actor, and Hollywood movie star Ronald Coleman, whom my mother adored. My father, believed the new baby brought good luck because the Kase family business was flourishing even during the post great depression period and the beginning of war in Europe. A few years ago, I began to examine the different stages of my life and remembered the good and not so good times, but my parents, who lived in good health into their 90s, were always there to listen to my troubles and celebrate my triumphs. I hope I have sufficiently passed on that support to my children and grandson. The other half of my great luck in life, is owed to Kathleen, and the other unusually caring and creative people whom I have featured in this book.

Ron Kase, is a sociologist, retired professor and university administrator, grant writer, local historian, author, husband, father, and grandfather, who lives in New Jersey the most democratically based, socially conscious state, in the nation. Where the First Amendment is celebrated, and practiced, and the Second Amendment is controlled, in order to protect everyone.

Contact: ronkase@rocketmail.com

Made in the USA
Middletown, DE
08 March 2025